Complete Guide to

REDUCING
ENERGY
COSTS

First Printing, September 2006

Copyright © by Consumers Union of United States Inc.,

Yonkers, N.Y. 10703

Published by Consumers Union of United States Inc., Yonkers, N.Y. 10703

ISBN = 1-933524-04-9

ISBN 13 = 978-1-933524-04-7

Manufactured in the United States of America

Text printed on paper containing minimum 30% post-consumer recycled fiber.

CONTENTS

■ ■ ■

20 FREE WAYS TO SAVE ENERGY

This book is crammed with ways to cut your energy bills. Some take a little money and effort, such as weatherstripping your windows. Some take a little restraint, such as picking a sedan instead of an SUV. Others require investment, such as choosing the more-efficient refrigerator, even if the price tag is a bit higher. Of course, the best ways to save energy dollars are the ones that take no money and little or no effort. That's what you'll find in this chapter—20 simple things you can do to start saving money right this minute, without having to reach for your wallet.

At the end of the chapter, you'll find another list that includes a few easy energy-saving ideas that don't cost more than a few dollars. These ideas are covered in more detail later in the book, but they are so cheap and easy, we couldn't resist including them here to make sure you don't miss them.

As the cost of heating your home and running your car continues to climb, we hope this book will help ease the burden on you and your family. And it's nice to know that saving energy does more than save you money: It helps save resources. Using less energy pollutes less, creates less acid rain, and results in less global warming. Even if you do nothing more than the 20 free things listed here, you will have made a difference in your budget and a difference in the world. Not bad for free.

1. Wash clothes in cold water. You might guess that most of the energy used by a washing machine goes into vigorously swishing the clothes around. In fact, about 90 percent of it is spent elsewhere, heating the water for the load. You can save substantially by washing and rinsing at cooler temperatures. Warm water helps the suds to get at the dirt, but cold-water detergents will work effectively for just about everything in the hamper.

2. Hang it up. Clotheslines aren't just a bit of backyard nostalgia. They really work, given a stretch of decent weather. You spare the energy

Most of the energy used in cleaning your clothes goes toward heating the water. Using cold-water soaps and cold water instead of warm or hot water will save you money.

a dryer would use, and your clothes will smell as fresh as all outdoors without the perfumes in fabric softeners and dryer sheets. You'll also get more useful life out of clothes dried on indoor or outdoor clotheslines—after all, dryer lint is nothing but your wardrobe in the process of wearing out.

3. Don't overdry your laundry. Clothes will need less ironing and hold up better if you remove them from the dryer while they're still just a bit damp. If you are in the market for a dryer, look for one with a moisture sensor; it will be less likely than thermostat-equipped models to run too long.

4. Let the dishwasher do the work. Don't bother prerinsing dishes with the idea that your dishwasher will work less hard. CONSUMER REPORTS has found that this added step can waste 20 gallons of heated water a day. All you need to do is scrape off leftover food. Enzyme-based detergents will help make sure the dishes emerge spotless.

5. Put your PC to sleep. Keep your computer and its monitor in sleep mode rather than leaving them on around the clock. You stand to use 80 percent less electricity, which over the course of a year could have the effect of cutting CO_2 emissions by up to 1,250 pounds, according to EPA estimates.

6. Turn down the heat in the winter, and turn down the cool in the summer. Lower the thermostat 5° to 10° F when you're sleeping or are out of the house. "A 10° decrease can cut your heating bill by as much as 20 percent," says Jim Nanni, manager of the appliance and home-improvement testing department of CONSUMER REPORTS. And before you put on a cotton sweater to ward off a slight chill from the AC in summer, consider that for every degree you raise the thermostat

Washing dishes by hand uses more water than using the dishwasher for the same number of dishes. Prerinsing the dishes before you load them in the dishwasher wastes water without getting them any cleaner.

setting, you can expect to cut your cooling costs by at least 3 percent.

7. A cold hearth for a warmer house. A conventional fireplace draws a small gale out of the room and sends it up the chimney. Assuming the indoor air has been warmed by your central heating system, that means your energy dollars are going up the chimney, too. Instead, consider a direct-vent, sealed-combustion gas fireplace. CONSUMER REPORTS has found that those units have an energy efficiency of about 70 percent—and the sight of the flames is a lot more warming than staring at a radiator. For more information, see "Fireplaces Waste Heat," page 38.

8. Lower the shades and raise the windows. Not at the same time, of course, but your windows and shades are great tools to help moderate temperatures in the home. Because of central air conditioning, we tend to forget these time-tested, traditional ways of making the house comfortable. Shades are particularly helpful in blocking the sun from west-facing rooms in the afternoon. At night, if the forecast calls for cooler temperatures and low humidity, give the AC a rest. Open windows upstairs and down, and use window fans or a whole-house fan.

9. Put a spin on home cooling. You can operate a couple of fans with a fraction of the electricity needed for air conditioning, and their cooling effect may make it possible to cut back on AC use.

10. Take care of your air conditioner, and it will take care of you. Your air conditioner will run more efficiently if you clean or replace its filter every other week during heaviest use. Keep leaves and other debris away from the central air's exterior condenser, and keep the condenser coils clean.

11. Spend less for hot water. Set the hot water heater at 120° F (or the "low" setting), which is

A roaring fire can leave you cold. The fire sucks more furnace heat up the chimney than it generates.

hot enough for most needs. If the tank feels warm to the touch, consider wrapping it with conventional insulation or a blanket made for that purpose. To help conserve the water's heat on its way to the faucets, insulate the plumbing with pipe sleeves; with these, you can raise the end-use temperature by 2° to 4° F.

12. Think twice before turning on the oven. Heating food in the microwave uses only 20 percent of the energy required by a full-sized oven. And while the second-hand heat from the oven may be welcome in winter, it can put an added load on your air conditioner in warmer months.

13. Use the right pan. When cooking on the stovetop, pick your pan, then put it on an element or burner that's roughly the same size. You'll use much less energy than you would with a mismatched burner and pan. Steam foods instead of

Match pan to burner size to save energy.

boiling. If you do boil, be sure to put a lid on the pot to make the water come to a boil faster.

14. Read the label. The EnergyGuide label, that is. When you shop for a new appliance, look for the label that gives an estimate of annual energy consumption. To help you make sense of that statistic, the label also states the highest and lowest figures for similar models.

15. Dust off the Crock-Pot. Slow cooking in a Crock-Pot uses a lot less energy than simmering on the stove.

Rediscover the Crock-Pot slow cooker. It uses less energy than a pot simmering on the stove.

16. Clean the coils on your refrigerator using a tapered appliance brush. Your fridge's motor won't have to run as long or as often. In addition to saving energy dollars, you'll prolong the life of the appliance. See "Refrigerator Maintenance," page 78.

> *If you travel at 65 mph instead of 55, you are penalized by lowering your mileage 12.5 percent.*

17. Drive steadily—and a bit slower. Hard acceleration and abrupt braking will use more fuel than if you start and slow more moderately. Keeping down your overall speed matters, too, because aerodynamic drag increases dramatically as you drive faster. If you travel at 65 mph instead of 55, you are penalized by lowering your mileage 12.5 percent. If you get your vehicle up to 75 mph, you're losing 25 percent compared with mileage at 55 mph.

18. Roof racks are a drag. Most cars are reasonably streamlined, but you work against their slipperiness if you carry things on the roof. A loaded roof rack can decrease an SUV's fuel efficiency by 5 percent, and that of a more aerodynamic car by 15 percent or more. Even driving with empty ski racks wastes gas.

19. Stick with regular. If your car's manufacturer specifies regular gas, don't buy premium with the thought of going faster or operating more efficiently. You'd be spending more with no benefit. Most cars have built-in sensors that adjust the engine timing to the gas in the tank. Even if the owner's manual recommends high-octane gas, ask the dealership about switching to regular.

20. No loitering. Don't let the engine run at idle any longer than necessary. After starting the car in the morning, begin driving right away; don't let it sit and "warm up" for several minutes. An engine actually warms up faster while driving. With most gasoline engines, it's more efficient to turn off the engine than to idle longer than 30 seconds.

AND IF YOU DON'T MIND SPENDING A FEW DOLLARS

1. A tighter home is a toastier home. Insulation is your home's first line of defense against the weather, right? Wrong. Before you bulk up with fiberglass blankets, seal the leaks. Inexpensive foam strips and caulking can cut your heating and cooling bills by 5 to 30 percent. For more on weather stripping see Chapter 2, Plugging the Leaks.

2. Try do-it-yourself low-E windows. If your windows don't have a low-E coating, consider applying a self-adhesive film on the glass. This treatment is a lot cheaper than replacing the units, and better-quality films are quite durable. For more on low-E coatings, both built-in and add-on, see "Gas, Glass, and Low-E Coatings," page 43.

3. Use a programmable thermostat. Roughly half of the typical home's energy bill goes for heating and cooling, according to the Department of Energy. The easiest way to save, short of sweating

or shivering, is to use programmable thermostats. They can pay for themselves in about a year. For more information, see "Quality Programming," page 100.

4. Switch to those funny-looking fluorescents. You may not be familiar with compact fluorescent lamps (CFLs), but give them a try. A single bulb can save from $25 to $45 over its life. And it's a long life: Manufacturers claim that CFLs last between 5 and 13 times longer than standard incandescent bulbs. For more information, see "Bright Choices: Compact Fluorescent Lamps," page 95.

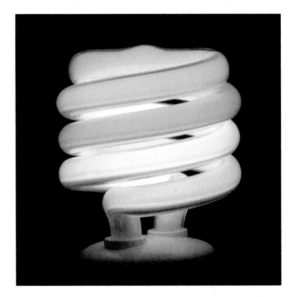

A compact fluorescent lamp produces as much light as an incandescent while using a fraction of the power.

PLUGGING THE LEAKS

Individual small air leaks in your home are easy to over-look, but collectively they can waste as much energy as leaving the front door wide open. By sealing the cracks and holes that riddle the typical home, you can save between 5 and 30 percent on your heating and cooling costs.

The good news is that once you sleuth out all the little leaks, they are easy to seal. You can do most of the work yourself, and the materials you'll need—foam strips, caulking, and the like—cost very little. No matter how well insulated, a home riddled with leaks is like a foam picnic cooler with the lid open. So seal up your house before you even think about adding insulation or making other expensive improvements such as replacing a furnace or central-air-conditioning unit.

Sealing your home's air leaks is an excellent investment. Caulking and weatherstripping can be expected to have a payback period of just one year, according to the Department of Energy. The exact savings will vary depending on the cost of the job, the amount of energy you've saved, and the current cost of the energy you use. But it isn't just a matter of dollars and cents. You also will feel better in a draft-free home. If a chilly breeze is wafting through a room, cranking up the thermostat won't make it go away. Sealing the leaks will.

When you are looking for leaks, poorly sealed doors and windows are the obvious culprits, but the problem is aggravated by something called the chimney effect. Warm air rises, keeping hot-air balloons aloft, or traveling up into your attic, as the case may be. The warm air escapes from the upper floors through cracks and holes. This creates lower air pressure in the home, which in turn draws cold

Storm windows help seal out winter winds. You can get a temporary seal with a kit that includes clear, heat-shrink plastic and double-sided tape. Put the tape around the outside edge of the moldings, stick the plastic to it, and then warm it with a hair dryer to shrink it and remove sags and wrinkles.

> " *Caulking and weatherstripping can be expected to have a payback period of just one year.* "

air in through leaks in the floors below. The result: You're living in a vertical wind tunnel. Sealing your home stops this flow of cold air.

FINDING THE LEAKS

Before you can seal your home's leaks, you have to find them, including the tiny ones that you probably overlook each day. You can hire professionals with special testing equipment to do the job (see "Should You Get an Energy Audit?," page 11). Or you can grab a clipboard and do your own room-to-room exam. It's a low-tech version of a professional audit, and while neither as expansive nor as expensive, it's a reliable way to find out where that cold air is coming from in the winter, and where it's going in the summer.

Down in the Basement

The most significant gaps tend to be down in the basement and up in the attic. Chances are that you don't spend most of your time at either level, but those are the areas that contribute most to the chimney effect. In a typical home, windows and doors in the main living areas account for just 15 percent or so of the overall infiltration.

Air is particularly apt to leak in along the top of the foundation wall, especially in older homes. In typical home construction, there will be a sill plate lying flat atop the wall and a rim joist standing upright on it. The most likely place for a leak in the basement is between those two, though you should check everywhere. When you are ready to seal the leak, clean the area well with a shop vacuum, and then caulk or apply expanding foam to seal the gaps. (For more on working with caulk and foam, see "Applying Caulk around Doors and Windows," page 18, and "Plugging Holes with Foam," page 20.) You may also want to insulate the top of the foundation wall as explained in Chapter 4, Insulation and Ventilation.

Up in the Attic

Before heading up to the attic, check to see whether the access hatch or door is well sealed. If access is through a hatch, you'll want to place foam weather stripping along the top of the stops that it rests on, and attach a square of solid foam insulation to the top of the hatch with construction adhesive. Install hooks and eyes to fasten the hatch so that it compresses the weather stripping when in place. If you enter the attic through a regular door, weather strip the edges as explained in "Installing Vinyl Tube Weather strips," page 32. Attach solid foam insulation to the back of the door with construction adhesive. Screw it in place with a drywall screw in each corner to hold the foam in place while the adhesive dries. In either case, make sure the adhesive is for use on foam insulation: Regular construction adhesive dissolves foam.

■ ■ ■ Insulating Folding Attic Stairs

1. To design your insulating box, measure both the opening and how far the stairs protrude into the attic when closed. Make the box big enough to sit on the attic floor if there is one, or on the framing if there is no floor. Cut long lengths of foam on the table saw, or by guiding a circular saw along a straight scrap of plywood screwed to both the foam and a sheet of plywood below it.

2. Cut pieces to length by guiding a utility knife repeatedly along the edge of a framing square, taking progressively deeper cuts. Fit the assembly together over the attic opening, and make any necessary adjustments. Glue the pieces together with construction adhesive made for foam board. Pin the corners together by pushing in nails to hold things together while you work. Clamp gently with bar clamps if you have them.

3. Cut a top to fit over the four sides, glue it in place using construction adhesive, and pin it together with nails. Tape fiberglass insulation to the top of the box with double-sided carpet tape. Put the box over the opening in the attic.

Folding attic stairs create a special problem when you're insulating because when folded, they protrude awkwardly above the attic floor. The Department of Energy recommends that you build a foam-board box that fits over both the stairs and the opening. (See "Insulating Folding Attic Stairs," page 9.) You can pull the box over the stairs as you leave the attic, and put it out of the way when you go back up. Apply some vinyl V-seal weather stripping along the bottom edge for a good seal. (If local code won't allow you to use foam board, substitute fibrous duct board, a pressed fiberglass board faced with foil and used for making heating vents.)

Once you're in the attic, look for openings around pipes, wires, and ductwork. When you seal them, use caulk or expanding foam, as explained in "Applying Caulk around Doors and Windows," page 18, and "Plugging Holes with Foam," page 20. Seal flues and chimneys with a high-temperature silicone caulk.

From Room to Room

Painters apply caulk along door and window moldings all the time to create a nice, smooth transition at the wall. You can do it to save energy. The gaps between the moldings and the wall lead outside, and even a small one can let in a lot of air: A gap of only $1/16$ inch adds up to the equivalent of a square-inch hole every 16 inches. To seal the gaps, apply a thin bead of paintable caulk in the corner formed by the molding and the wall. Put on a disposable latex glove, and smooth out the caulk with your finger. Caulk around heating and cooling vents, too. If you

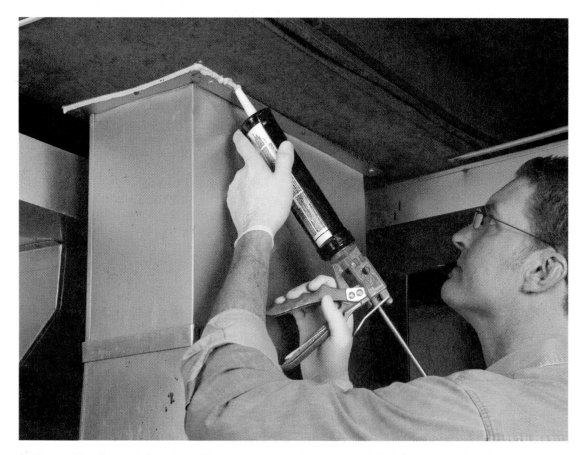

Seal around heating vents in unheated basements to keep heated or cooled air from leaking into the basement.

can remove the register, caulk around the back near the edge to seal out air leaking from the floor or wall. If you can't remove the register, caulk the seam where the vent meets the wall.

Make a note of outlets and switches on exterior and interior walls, and buy gaskets to seal them, as explained in "Sealing Outlets and Switches," page 16.

In the kitchen, look under the sink for gaps around the pipes. You can seal the smaller ones with caulk and the larger ones with foam. Caulk the perimeter of the kitchen and bath exhaust fans, if possible. In bathrooms, also seal around any pipes.

Air can leak in around outlets, baseboards, and even medicine cabinets mounted in an exterior wall. Seal around the medicine cabinet with caulk the same way you would caulk around a window; seal outlets and switches with a foam gasket as explained in "Sealing Outlets and Switches," page 16.

The point where baseboards meet the wall and the floor is another spot where leaks are common. Caulk will seal the leaks, but before caulking, take a peek at what's behind the wall, with a mind to adding insulation if it's lacking. Carefully pry off a section of baseboard, and

use a keyhole saw or utility knife to make a small inspection hole where the trim covers the lower wall. If there's no insulation, see "Where to Insulate," page 67.

■ ■ ■ Should You Get an Energy Audit?

A home energy audit can save you plenty of trouble and money by pinpointing just where your house leaks. A professional audit looks at just about everything in the house, but there are two main components. First, the audit company puts a calibrated blower, called a blower door, in one of your entry doors. The blower blows air out of the house, sucking air through the leaks, so they can assess how much leakage there is. Second, a complete audit will include an infrared photograph of your home that shows the temperature of the home's surfaces so that you can identify areas where heat is escaping.

Typically the audit will look for a wide range of problems and make a wide range of recommendations—more insulation, weather stripping, storm windows, insulating blinds, furnace tune-ups or replacement with a more-efficient furnace, recalibrating the thermostat, putting a timer on the water heaters, and so on. The more complete the audit, the more detail it will have and the more recommendations it's likely to make.

An exhaustive audit from a commercial company can be expensive, but you can save money by getting an audit without all the bells and whistles. Check the phonebook, and compare prices and services. Check with your utility company, too—it may offer a free or low-cost audit. Also check with your state's energy department to learn whether you might be reimbursed for all or part of the cost of a professional audit.

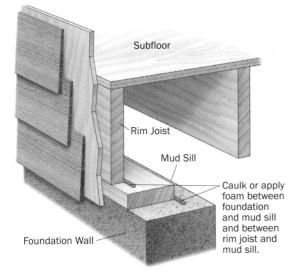

Subfloor

Rim Joist

Mud Sill

Caulk or apply foam between foundation and mud sill and between rim joist and mud sill.

Foundation Wall

Caulk around the foundation to seal air leaks.

DOING YOUR OWN ENERGY EXAM

When pros do a complete energy audit, they'll look at everything right down to your thermostat. But the first layer of problems—the ones that cost you the most money—are also the most obvious ones. Do you have or need double-pane windows or storm windows? Do you have insulation in the attic, in the walls, and around the foundation? Do you have or need weather stripping? Are the holes in the house for wires and pipes adequately sealed? You can probably conduct that kind of audit without leaving your chair.

When it comes to finding leaks, the pros quantify those leaks by exaggerating them with a blower that sucks air into your house—something you can't do from your chair. You can do much the same job with fans and by choosing a windy day to do the exam. A good wind has the effect of drawing heated or cooled air out of the home, making leaks easier to find.

Start your exam by closing all exterior doors, windows, and fireplace flues. Turn off any appliance that burns gas, including the furnace, water heater, and stove, to prevent problems with fumes or leaking gas. Turn on all exhaust fans, including a whole-house attic fan if you have one. If you have window fans, turn them on, too, positioned to blow air out of the house. Pinpoint the leaks by burning a stick of incense and holding it near windows, doors, and exterior walls. The smoke will change direction in the presence of a leak; move the incense back and forth to pinpoint the exact location.

Examining the Exterior

Sealing the leaks on the inside of the wall doesn't mean you can ignore leaks on the outside of the wall. If air can get inside the wall, it can find a way to get inside your house, too. Walk around the outside of your house and look for gaps and

Leaky windows create drafts. You can pinpoint the source by holding an incense stick near a suspected leak, and watching for changes in the plume of smoke.

> *Sealing the leaks on the inside of the wall doesn't mean you can ignore leaks on the outside of the wall.*

holes. Give particular attention to areas where two different building materials meet—the top of the foundation, alongside chimneys, and the transition between types of siding. Here is a checklist of other potential trouble spots:

■ Entry holes for telephone, TV, and electric lines, and gas- and water-supply lines

■ Exterior light fixtures

■ Dryer vents

■ Furnace fuel pipes

■ Door frames, window frames, and around the edges of permanently installed storm windows

Rope caulk is basically putty in a string and applies easily. It also removes easily when it's time to take out removable storms. On permanent storms, like this one, just leave the putty in place.

Compute Your Weatherproofing Payback

The U.S. Department of Energy offers a Home Energy Saver auditing tool that helps you estimate the payback period for various weatherproofing projects. You begin by entering your ZIP code, then supply the payback period you'd like, the size of your home, the number of windows, the current price you pay for heating fuel, and so on. The site will suggest energy-saving changes you might make, along with a projection of how much you stand to save in energy and dollars. There's even an estimate of how these measures would reduce pollution.

Get to the site by going to *www.Consumer Reports.org/energy*, and clicking on Home Energy Audit.

ConsumerReports.org/energy

Use exterior-rated caulk to seal holes and cracks that are up to $\frac{1}{4}$ inch wide. To fill larger gaps, you can use either polyurethane or latex foam. The cured foam can be painted so that it blends in with the home's exterior, and which also will protect the material from the degrading effects of ultraviolet light. If you want to paint the caulk, make sure before you apply it that it is labeled as paintable. When sealing around storm windows that you remove after each winter, you may want to use preformed strips of putty, called caulking cord or rope caulk. You press the strip of putty into the opening between the storm and the window. When you take the windows down in the spring, the putty peels away easily.

> " *You press the strip of putty into the opening between the storm and the window.* "

■ ■ ■ An After-Dark Audit

At night, try spotting larger gaps by having someone outside shine a flashlight or trouble light around the doors. If you can see the light from the inside, you're looking at a leak.

A WEATHERIZING ARSENAL

Hardware stores and home centers carry an amazing variety of products for sealing the home, although you can't expect the shelves to be quite so well-stocked once warm weather approaches. To simplify matters, keep in mind that there are two basic types of material. The first, weather stripping, is used to make a seal around operable parts, such as window sashes and doors. The second type—including caulk, foam, and putty—is used to fill up gaps in walls, around trim, and the like.

Weather Stripping

When you close a window or a door, you may think you're shutting out the elements. But unless something seals the door or window at the edges, it can leak a considerable amount of air. Weather stripping provides that seal.

Some types of weather stripping are installed permanently with nails or screws. Others are self-adhesive and can be easily applied and removed. Temporary installation (such as plastic-film "storms" stretched over a window) makes sense if you don't need a certain product year-round or if you are renting your home. One limitation of self-adhesive weather stripping is that the surface must be clean before you apply it; wash the area with water, and then wipe it down with a cloth dampened in alcohol. Let it dry before you apply the weather stripping. The adhesive is less effective in cold weather as well, so installation is best done when the temperature is above 50° F.

Here's a rundown of what's available:

■ Foam and felt strips come in rolls. They can be cut to length with scissors, and they install easily with their peel-off adhesive backing.

> *When you close a window or a door, you may think you're shutting out the elements. But unless something seals the door or window at the edges, it can leak a considerable amount of air.*

Note that these strips can become compressed with use, and should be replaced when they no longer spring back to an effective thickness.

■ Tubular rubber and vinyl strips usually are self-adhesive, although some have a flange through which you drive staples or brads. Many exterior-door thresholds come with a tubular strip to make a good seal with the door.

■ Vinyl tension strips are self-adhesive and look like long V-shaped hinges. They fold when a door or window is closed and flex to fit tightly against the other side of the opening. Metal strips come both as V-strips and as a flatter single-layer piece. Both types tack in place.

Caulk, Foam, and Putty

Caulk, foam, and putty typically are used to seal holes that were made intentionally, such as those for electrical, plumbing, and ventilation systems, as well as cracks that have opened up over time, such as those between a window and the siding.

■ Caulk is a sealant that comes in toothpaste-like tubes or in larger cartridges that require a caulk gun for application. Silicone caulks and silicone-modified polymer caulks are weatherproof and long-

Seal doors and windows with weather stripping. From left to right, nail vinyl gaskets around doors. Unroll vinyl V-strip, fold it in half, and stick it to door and window jambs. Felt presses against doors to seal them. Metal weather strip fits in the door opening. Install foam snugly against the moving parts of doors and windows and to the top and bottom of the window sash.

Weather stripping Compared				
Type of Weatherstripping	**Best Use**	**Relative Cost**	**Advantage**	**Disadvantage**
Vinyl V-strip	Double-hung windows; top and sides of doors	Moderate	Easy to install; durable; out of sight when installed	Surfaces must be clean, flat, and smooth; may slightly impede operation of door or window.
Felt	Fitted against doors or windows	Low	Inexpensive	Least effective at preventing airflow; low durability; high visibility.
Foam	Top and bottom of window sash; doorjambs; attic hatches	Low	Installation extremely easy	Low durability. Check package for length of guarantee.
Tubular rubber and vinyl	Doors	Moderate to high	Effective air barrier	Highly visible. Self-stick may not adhere to metal.

Source: U.S. Department of Energy

lasting and have good flexibility, but they're more expensive than other caulks. You should also check the label to see whether or not you can paint over them. Latex caulks are smooth and easier to apply than silicone but are less flexible. They should be protected with paint if used outdoors.

■ Backer rod is a foam strip used to fill cracks wider than $3/8$ inch and deeper than $1/2$ inch prior to caulking. Insert backer rod by pushing it into place with a screwdriver or putty knife.

■ Rope caulk is a preformed puttylike cord that can be removed when no longer needed, as is the case if you want to seal storm windows only for the winter. Note that oil-based rope caulk may stain woodwork.

■ Expanding foam comes in aerosol form, something like whipped cream. Polyurethane foam expands so dramatically that it can distort window and doorjambs if injected into

voids between the frame and the structural rough opening. Latex foam expands less, is somewhat easier to control, and is much easier to clean up.

Use caulk, foam, and putty to seal around nonmoving parts. From left to right, fill large cracks with backer rod before caulking. Seal holes with expanding foam, and use caulk to seal cracks. Caulk rope is a puttylike substance that tears into long, narrow strips and also seals cracks.

Sealing Outlets and Switches

Electrical outlets and switches might not be an obvious source of infiltration, but collectively outlets and switches can leak a significant amount of air. Even outlets and switches on interior walls contribute to the chimney effect and should be sealed.

Air very easily drifts though the electrical box and out the opening in the drywall or plaster. Hardware stores and home centers carry foam gaskets that cover the electrical box within the wall and are concealed by the cover plate.

Foam gaskets that fit behind the cover plates seal off drafts that come through outlets and switch boxes.

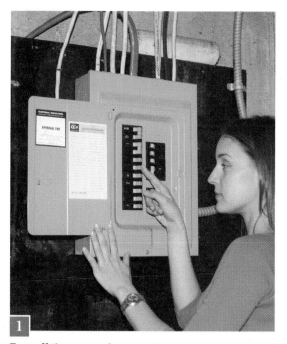

1

Turn off the power. Go to the fuse panel or breaker box and turn off the power to the circuit you are dealing with. Test that the circuit is off by plugging in a reliable lamp and seeing whether it will light.

2

Remove the cover plate. Plates are held in place by one or more screws. Remove the screws and lift off the plate.

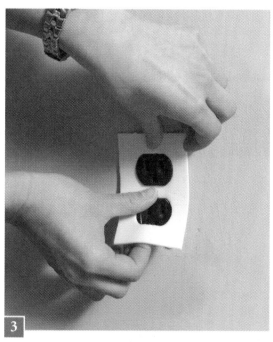

3

Install the gasket. Place a foam gasket over the electrical box, removing the punched-out holes in the foam for the outlets or switch. Replace the cover.

4

Block the slots. Even the slots in an outlet have a chilling effect. Insert child-safety plugs to block outlets that aren't in use.

Applying Caulk around Doors and Windows

You use caulk to seal leaks both inside and outside the house. Outside, you'll caulk between the window moldings and house. Inside, you'll caulk around window and door trim.

For larger jobs like this, you'll want to use a caulk gun instead of the toothpastelike tubes. The gun has a large trigger that you squeeze to drive a plunger into the back of the cartridge, forcing caulk out the front. To save a partially emptied cartridge, use the cap that came with it (if one did) or place plastic wrap around the tip and secure it with a rubber band. Use leftover caulk as soon as possible because it has a short shelf life once opened.

Cut the top off the nozzle. Slice off the tip of the cartridge nozzle with a utility knife. (You may find it easier to apply caulk if the tip is cut at a 45-degree angle.) The more of the tip you remove, the larger the bead of caulk will be. The hole should be the same size as the cracks you're filling—$^3/_{16}$ inch in diameter is about average.

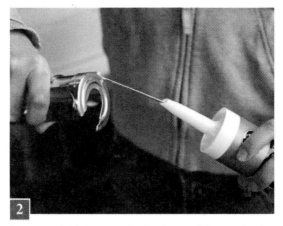

Puncture the inner seal. Push a long nail (or the pivoting metal rod attached to the bottom of some guns) into the nozzle to break the plastic seal inside.

Put the cartridge in the gun. To insert the cartridge, turn the plunger so its teeth face up and pull back the plunger at the back of the gun. Put in the cartridge, push the plunger forward, and then turn the teeth face down.

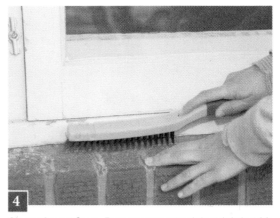

Clean the surface. Remove any remaining debris with a wire brush if the surface is masonry; use a bristle brush if the surface is wood or vinyl. Then wash the surface with water, wipe with alcohol, and let dry.

Apply caulk. Hold the gun at roughly a 45-degree angle to the work, and push it along rather than pull it, if possible. Pushing will help force the caulk into the joint.

5 **Mask off adjoining areas.** For a neat edge along a caulked joint, run painter's tape along each side of the area. Paintable silicone caulk in particular is runny, and masking with painter's tape keeps the job from getting messy.

Work your way along the seam. Squeeze the trigger to advance the plunger and gradually force out the caulk. Caulk will continue to come out after applying pressure, so stop squeezing before reaching the end of a run. Disengage the plunger at the end of the run.

8 **Smooth out the caulk.** Smooth the caulk by running a plastic spoon along the bead.

9 **Remove the tape.** Pull the tape off the window or door immediately, before the caulk has a chance to dry.

Plugging Holes with Foam

You can fill holes in walls with caulk, but expanding spray foam does the job more quickly and also offers insulation value. It is especially useful for filling hollow spots in the wall, particularly around plumbing and vent stacks. Note that polyurethane foam sticks stubbornly to anything it contacts before curing, including your skin. To remove it, promptly use acetone as a solvent. (Some fingernail-polish removers contain acetone and can be used for this purpose. You can also buy pure acetone at most hardware stores.) Latex foam is water-soluble, which means you can clean it up with soap and water. If left exposed, however, both foams are vulnerable to weather; so paint any foam that will be visible once the job is done.

Make a trial run. Wear old clothes, disposable plastic gloves, and protective eyewear when applying the foam. Protect nearby surfaces with newspaper or drop cloths. Attach the nozzle, and shake the can as directed. Make a trial run with the foam, spraying it onto newspaper to see how much comes out and how much it expands.

Apply the foam. Hold the container as straight up and down as possible, and pull the trigger. Polyurethane gradually doubles in size as it dries, so fill the cavity about halfway, or as recommended. Latex foam expands less, and you can fill the cavity about 90 percent of the way, or as recommended.

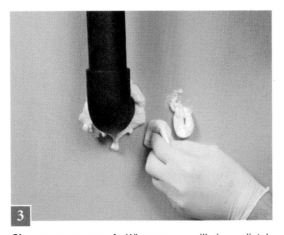

Clean up as you work. Wipe up any spills immediately with the recommended solvent. In most cases, this will be acetone for urethane foam, and water for latex foam.

Trim off the excess. Once the foam has hardened, trim off any excess with a utility knife, kitchen knife, or handsaw.

WEATHERPROOFING WINDOWS

Windows are especially vulnerable to the vagaries of climate and weather. You can reduce heat loss (or heat gain from sunny summer windows) with a few simple steps. To help curb radiant heat loss, get in the habit of drawing shades, blinds, and drapes at night. Do the same to block unwelcome sunlight. Also, consider taking advantage of solar warmth by opening coverings on southern-facing windows on sunny winter days. If you're due for new window treatments, consider buying insulating curtains that are quilted or foam-backed.

Remove window air conditioners at summer's end, too. They also produce cold air in the winter—not electrically, but by admitting chilly outdoor air. You need a good, strong back to lug around any but the smallest units. Instead of removing an air conditioner, you can buy an insulated cover for the exterior of the air conditioner. For an even better seal, install an interior cover made for the purpose, too. A problem with using covers is that the unit's evaporator pan can act as a petri dish for mold and mildew if water is allowed to sit in it. Have someone help you slide the air conditioner chassis from its shell and then soak up any water from the pan with a sponge. If the air conditioner doesn't slide out of a shell, let it dry out for a week before covering it.

■ ■ ■ Third Line of Defense

There should be two panes of glass between you and the outdoors—whether it's a single pane and a storm or a double-paned window with argon inside. No matter how good the glass, however, energy will always radiate from the warm side to the cold side—warmth escapes during cold weather and invades during hot weather. Close your drapes at night during cold weather to help keep heat in; close them during the day in the summer to help keep heat out.

■ ■ ■ Seal Older Casement Windows with Metal Weather Stripping

Casement windows go in and out of style. Modern ones usually come with good weatherstripping and insulated glass. Older windows had metal weather stripping like that on the window shown below, but no weather stripping lasts forever. If your casement window leaks, check the weather stripping. If it's vinyl and is leaking, contact the manufacturer for a replacement and directions. If it's metal and is in good shape, run a screwdriver between the jamb and the weatherstrip. This pushes the unattached edge out, which may be enough to solve the problem. If it doesn't, remove the old weather stripping and install a new metal weather strip.

You'll install the new strip the same way you install it on a door: Cut it to length with some tinsnips and nail the knurled edge to the jamb, spacing the nails 2 or 3 inches apart. The big difference: On a door, there are only three edges to seal. On a casement window, there are four—top, bottom, and two sides. For more on installing metal weatherstripping, see "Sealing a Door with Metal Weatherstrip," page 34.

Sealing a Double-Hung Window with V-Seal Weather Strips

Vinyl V-seal weatherstrips are strips about 1 inch wide that you fold in half to form a V. When you put them in place on the window frame, the V is between the window and frame, where it opens up to close the gap. The vinyl is easy to cut, easy to apply, and more durable than foam.

Vinyl strips are self-adhesive, but if you want them to stay put, you have to clean whatever you stick them to. Soap leaves a slippery film, and self-adhesive strips won't stick very well to that, either. Wipe down the surface with a wet rag to remove most of the dirt; then wipe again with denatured alcohol. The alcohol picks up any leftover dirt and helps the water evaporate so you can get to work almost immediately.

1 **Clean the surfaces.** Before you install the tape, clean the surfaces of the window that you'll attach the tape to. Wash them with water, wipe with alcohol, and let the surfaces dry. Test the alcohol on a small area first to make sure it doesn't damage a natural-wood finish. You'll need to wash the channels that the window travels in, as well as the back of the rail that holds the lock, the top of the upper sash, and the bottom of the lower sash.

2 **Weather strip the top of the top window.** Lowering the sash gives you access to its top rail. Cut a strip to the length of the rail, and fold it in half along the prescored line. Remove the backing from the self-stick adhesive, and press the weather stripping to the top of the top rail.

Weather strip the bottom of the bottom window. Raise the lower sash and attach a strip to the underside of its bottom rail.

Weather strip the middle rail. Cut a strip for the middle of the window, attaching it to the face of the upper sash's lock rail so that it will be compressed when the window is closed. In this case, the point of the V should face up, to make operating the window easier.

Weather strip the sides of the window. Cut a strip 3 or 4 inches longer than the height of the window opening. Slide the bottom sash all the way up, and stick the V-strip in the channel normally occupied by the closed window. Repeat on the other side of the window; then lower both windows and put V-strip in the channels that hold the upper sash. If there is a sash rope or chain with counterweights, install the V-strip somewhere in the channel where it won't interfere.

Resetting or Replacing a Windowpane

Older windows can be problems. Panes crack, the putty dries out and falls off, the panes start rattling—those are all sure signs that air has found yet another way to work its way into your house. To reset or replace a pane in a wooden window, you'll need window putty, a hair dryer, glazier's points that hold the pane in place, some boiled linseed oil, and a few tools. If it's a newer window, especially one with thermopanes, contact the manufacturer to find out how to make the repair.

Take out the putty before removing broken glass, and wear heavy gloves.

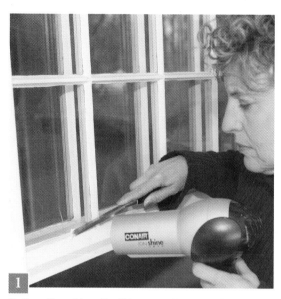

Soften the old putty. Warm up the putty with a hair dryer to soften it and make it easier to remove.

Remove the old putty. Scrape away all of the old putty with a chisel. Thoroughly clean the wooden channel where the putty will go, sanding over it lightly with fine sandpaper if necessary.

Remove the glazier's points. If you're replacing the pane, pull out the glazier's points with needle-nose pliers. Put on a pair of gloves and carefully push the broken glass from the opening. If you're just replacing dried-out putty, leave the glazier's points alone.

Seal the bare wood. New putty won't stick to old, dry wood because the wood sucks the moisture out of the putty. Paint the window channel with boiled linseed oil to keep this from happening. If you need a replacement pane, measure from the side of one channel to the side of the other. Have the hardware store cut the glass $\frac{1}{8}$ inch smaller in width and in height.

5

Apply putty to the frame. Roll some putty between your hands to create a thin line of putty. Line the channels with the putty, and push it against the frame with a putty knife.

6

Install the glass. Put the glass in the opening, and push it into the putty, seating it gently but firmly.

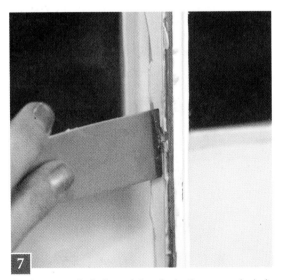

7

Apply new glazier's points. Push the new glazier's points in place with a putty knife until the flange seats against the wood. Put points in roughly every 4 inches around the window.

8

Putty the window. Warm a ball of putty in your hands, then form it into a thin rope that is the width of the channel. Apply the putty around the channel, pushing firmly in place with your fingers. Dip the putty knife in the linseed oil so that it won't stick to the putty. Smooth out the putty with the knife, forming a neat bevel in the process. Pull off any extra putty. When the putty has dried, paint it to match the sash.

Replacing a Threshold Gasket

Installing weathertight thresholds, which have a rubber gasket that presses against the door to seal out the heat and cold, is tricky and best left to a carpenter. In contrast, replacing a worn gasket on an existing threshold is about as simple as it gets. (If you don't have a weathertight threshold, install a door sweep, as explained on page 28.) On wooden thresholds, you usually just pull out the gasket, fit in a new one, and cut it to length with a knife. On metal thresholds like the one shown here, you usually need to remove the threshold to remove the gasket.

Unscrew the threshold. Metal thresholds are screwed to the floor. Remove the screws. Pry up the threshold, being careful not to damage the doorjambs.

Remove the rubber gasket. Twist the tabs underneath the threshold to align them with the slots. The tabs are part of a bar that the gasket is mounted on. Remove the bar and gasket. If there are no tabs, pull the gasket off the threshold with a pair of pliers.

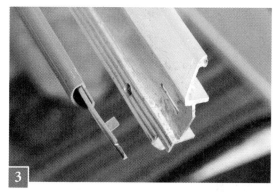

Fit the tabs in the threshold. Fit the tabs of the new gasket through the slots in the threshold. Twist the tabs with a pair of pliers to lock the gasket in place.

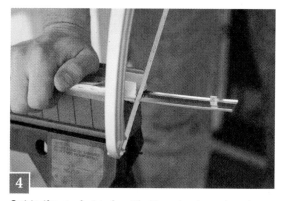

Cut to the gasket to length. Use a hacksaw to cut gaskets mounted on a tabbed metal bar. Cut unmounted gaskets to length with a utility knife.

Reattach the threshold. Screw the threshold back in place using the original screws and holes.

Installing a Door Sweep

The bottom of the door has to be treated differently from the sides and top because it doesn't meet a stop. Thresholds, which are available with some type of weather stripping, can be difficult to install. You not only need to cut them to length, you need to cut them to fit around doorjambs and door stops. It's a fussy job, one best left to the pros or to homeowners with solid do-it-yourself experience. Door sweeps, on the other hand, perform the same function as a weathertight threshold, and are easy to install. You cut the piece to length with a hacksaw, then screw it to the door. Some sweeps install on the outside of the door, and some install on the inside; no matter where they mount, they do a good job of keeping air from coming in under the door.

A low door sweep can abrade an adjacent carpet and also make it difficult to swing the door. You can buy a retractable sweep that automatically rises out of the way as the door opens. Those sweeps typically will work with a gap of up to $1/2$ inch between the bottom edge of the door and the threshold.

1

Measure the opening. If there is an old door sweep, remove it. Before buying a new sweep, measure the width of the door and also the gap between the door bottom and the threshold or floor below the door when closed. Shop for a sweep that will handle those distances.

Cut to length. Read the instructions for the new sweep to see whether its flange is mounted on the inside or outside of the door. Mark the length on the sweep. Remove the brush or vinyl flap, then cut the sweep with a hacksaw. Reinsert the sweep and cut it to length with a utility knife.

Lay out the screw holes. Hold the sweep in place so that its brush or flap makes good contact with the threshold or floor, and then mark the door for pilot holes.

Drill holes for the screws. Drill pilot holes for the screws. The holes should be roughly the diameter of the screws minus the thread, something that you can gauge by holding the screw next to the shank of the drill. Screw the sweep into place. If it has slotted holes, you'll be able to slightly adjust its position before fully driving the screws.

Sealing a Door with Foam Weather Strips

Doors rank with windows as energy-squandering parts of the house, typically answering for 11 percent of the wasted heat overall. A mere $1/8$-inch gap under an outside door will admit as much cold air as a 4-inch-diameter hole drilled right through the wall. A few feet of weather stripping keeps that air inside.

Foam weather stripping is one of the easiest kinds of weather stripping to install, though it's not the most durable. The one difficulty is that because the foam stretches during installation, it can be difficult to cut a piece the right length. The best way to measure is to stick one end of the strip in place and leave the backing on the rest of the strip. The backing keeps the strip from stretching, and you can then hold the strip in place and make the cut exactly where you want it.

1

Wash the surfaces. Self-adhesive weather strip won't stick to a dirty surface. Wash the surface with water, wipe it down with alcohol, and let it dry.

2 **Start on the latch side.** Begin peeling the backing from a strip, and attach the top, but no more, along the latch side of the door opening. Position it on the stop where the door will compress it. (The stop is the part of the frame against which the door closes.)

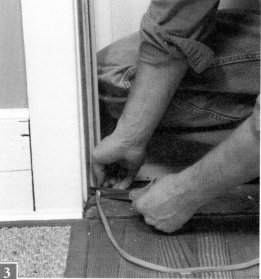

3 **Cut to length.** Cut the strip to length with scissors, remove the backing, and press the foam into place along the entire length of the latch side.

4 **Weatherstrip the top of the frame.** Apply a strip to the stop along the top of the frame the same way you applied it along the latch side.

5 **Weatherstrip the hinge side.** Along the side with hinges, apply the strip to the doorjamb next to the stop, where it will be compressed by the door when closed.

Installing Vinyl Tube Weather Strips

Vinyl-tube weather stripping nails to the door stops on the outside of the door, and it's an effective air barrier. While these tubes are more visible than vinyl V-strips, they're likely to last longer, too—the vinyl is much thicker, and it isn't constantly folding and unfolding as you open and close the door.

There are both self-stick and nail-on versions of tube weather stripping. The self-stick looks like it might be easier to install, but it can be hard to work one section of the weather strip into position without inadvertently sticking another section in the wrong place. Nail-on tubes are relatively simple to install if you use an awl, as shown here, to poke a clearance hole through the vinyl, and to make a dimple in the wood where the nail will go. If you buy a nail-on gasket, buy brass brads to attach it, too—they're not included with the gasket.

Gasket material comes in white, brown, or black—if your door or door stops are another color, you might want to consider a different weather-stripping system—the vinyl should not be painted.

1

Cut the gasket to length. Measure across the top of the door, and cut the gasket to length with a pair of scissors.

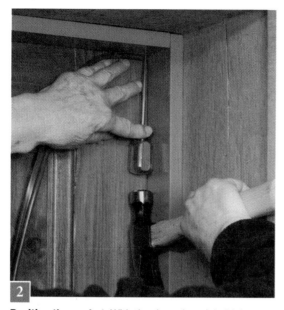

Position the gasket. With the door closed, hold the gasket in place with the point of an awl. Tap the awl with a hammer to poke through the gasket and make a slight indentation in the door stop.

Nail the gasket in place. Put a nail through the hole you made with the awl, and into the indentation in the wood. Hold with needle-nose pliers, if necessary, and drive the nail until the head is flush with the gasket. Push the awl through the gasket and into the wood roughly every 4 inches, and nail the gasket in place.

Cut a notch in the tube. Before you nail the side pieces in place, cut a notch in the tube so that the side gasket will nest against the top gasket.

Nail side gaskets in place. Start with the remaining piece of gasket; nail it in place at the top and work your way down the door, using the awl the same way you did on the top gasket. Drive nails into the strip every 4 to 6 inches. Cut the strip to length once you've nailed the entire piece in place. Repeat on the other side.

Sealing a Door with a Metal Weather Strip

Metal tension strips can be a good choice for exterior doors because they are less vulnerable to wet and cold weather than felt and foam strips are. While metal is more durable, it is a bit harder to install. You'll need tin snips instead of scissors, and you'll drive nails instead of popping a self-adhesive strip in place. If you've got a hammer and have ever used tin snips, you can do the job.

Lay out where the weather strip will go. Draw a line showing where the back of the weather stripping should go. The package will tell you where that is; in this case it's 1½ inches from the door stop. A combination square will help you draw a consistent line.

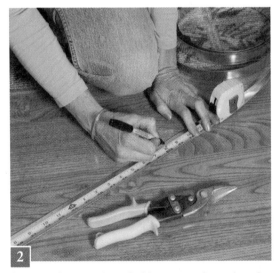

Cut the pieces to length. Measure and use tin snips to cut a piece long enough to go across the top door-jamb. Cut the remaining piece in half. You'll trim the sides to exact length later.

Attach the side. Put the strip along the latch jamb so that the narrow flat surface is against the line. Nail the top in place. Use a pair of needle-nose pliers to hold the nail so that you can drive it without hitting your fingers.

Pull the weather strip tight. Poke an awl into the bottom of the strip, pull the metal taut, then tap the awl into the doorjamb. Nail the bottom of the strip in place. Align the middle of the strip with the line, and nail it in place. Drive a nail every 2 inches to hold the strip in place.

Cut the side to length. Cut off the excess at the bottom with a pair of tin snips. Nail the bottom of the weather strip in place so it doesn't curl up and catch in the door.

Install the top and second side. Nail the second side in place the same way you installed the first. Install the weather stripping along the top, too, first nailing one end in place, then pulling it taut with the awl, and nailing the strip in place every 2 inches.

Cut the strip over the latch holes. Some of the weather strip will have covered up the holes in the jamb for the door latch. Cut away any of the strip that interferes with locking the door, and nail down any loose ends. Run a screwdriver between the jamb and weather stripping to pull it slightly away from the jamb.

Sealing Ductwork

It's worthwhile to seal and insulate ducts that pass through both unheated and uncooled areas of the home, such as the attic, garage, and crawl spaces. In tests at the Oak Ridge National Laboratory, taking this step cut household energy consumption by an average of 16 percent, and the U.S. Department of Energy calculates a payback period of less than three years. There's also the risk that leaky ducts will pick up pollutants from the basement or crawl spaces and broadcast them throughout the house.

Keep in mind that a blanket of insulation doesn't make a good seal. Ducts can be leaking under that bulky jacket, as you may be able to tell by a few signs: A room will seem uncomfortably warm or chilly. There may be little airflow at some registers. Or you may have noticed that your energy use has gone up markedly. An HVAC (heating, ventilation, and air-conditioning) contractor can check out the home's ducting using specialized equipment to test for leaks and then seal them. Your state may offer a financial incentive for having a certified contractor do the work. Or, if the ducts are accessible, you may want to take on the job of sealing them yourself.

If you do the job yourself, pay particular attention to joints between pieces of ductwork and corners. You may be able to detect air leaking out by simply feeling for it. Or, for a visual indicator, hold a lightweight piece of tissue to the suspected leak and see whether an air current moves it. Remove old insulation as necessary, wearing an OSHA-approved respirator or dust mask and a long-sleeved shirt as protection from the fiberglass.

Seal the gaps. Use spray foam or caulk to seal gaps where ducts pass through the floor or ceiling. This will keep cold basement or crawl-space air from working its way into your house.

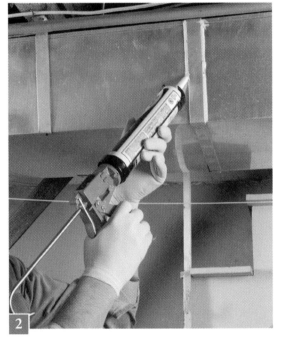

Apply duct mastic. Don't rely on the familiar gray fabric duct tape (even though the installers of your system may have done so); it isn't durable and is especially prone to drying out at high temperatures. Start instead by applying mastic—a glue designed to hold duct tape—on any leaks wider than $1/4$ inch.

Apply fiberglass tape. Apply fiberglass tape over the mastic to reinforce it. Apply a second coat of mastic, this one on top of the tape, and spread it with a putty knife. This combination of mastic and fiberglass tape is used instead of duct tape, which begins to leak after a short time.

Install the insulation. Use a product with an R-value of between 8 and 11, depending on the temperature extremes in your area and the space the duct is in. For example, air-conditioning ducts in a hot attic need more insulation than AC ducts in a cool basement. Reuse old insulation if it's in good shape, or install new batts of fiberglass insulation intended for use around ducts. Install the foil side out.

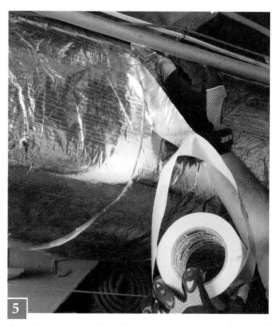

Tape the seams. Tape the seams between pieces of insulation to help hold them in place and minimize any air leakage. Use foil tape, rather than plastic or fabric duct tape. Plastic and fabric deteriorate and will spring leaks with time.

A HOUSE HAS TO BREATHE

Even a well-sealed home has to admit some air. After all, you and your pets need oxygen to breathe. Furnaces, gas water heaters, and fireplaces consume air. Exhaust fans require household air to do their work, as does a vented clothes dryer. That's not a problem in many homes. In fact, an older house with inadequate weatherproofing typically leaks four or five times more air than is needed. But if you plan on tightening up your house, indoor air quality may become an issue for a couple of reasons.

First, household-generated pollutants will be trapped, making them more hazardous. These include gases put out by particleboard, new carpeting, aerosol sprays, and certain cleaning products. Fuel-burning appliances may be emitting carbon monoxide if they aren't operating properly. Before sealing the house, have technicians check combustion appliances to ensure that they won't be producing this colorless, odorless gas. Install carbon-monoxide alarms in any room having a source of combustion, and on each level of the home.

You can reduce household pollutants in other ways. When possible, use aerosol sprays and volatile chemicals outside of the house, or at least have an exhaust fan nearby. New carpets may put off irritating fumes, and you can ask the dealer to unroll them for a few days before delivery; if that's not possible, plan on having the carpet installed during mild weather so that you can leave the room's windows open for a couple of days.

If you are in a region where radon gas is a potential problem, find out how to have your home tested. Nationwide, nearly 1 home in 15 has high levels of radon, and the gas has been identified as second only to smoking as a cause of lung cancer. For more information, contact your state health department or the National Radon Information Line at 800-767-7236.

■ ■ ■ Too Much of a Good Thing

Houses have always relied on a little bit of air leakage for a supply of fresh air. Occasionally a house is so well-sealed that it doesn't get enough fresh air. It's unlikely that retrofitting a leaky house with weather stripping, caulk, and foam will make your house that airtight. If you begin to notice condensation on the walls or constantly on the windows, however, you've done too good a job—call in a heating, ventilation, and air-conditioning contractor to discuss possible solutions.

■ ■ ■ Fireplaces Waste Heat

There's nothing like a blazing fireplace to create an aura of coziness in a home. But that coziness is deceptive. A blazing fire sucks a tremendous amount of heat up the flue. Once the fire is out, air still travels up the flue, even after you close the damper.

If you really want a fire in the fireplace, wait until those moderately cool nights when you're not running the heat. In the meantime, block the flue so heat can't escape up the chimney. Cut a plug out of rigid-foam insulation, put it in place, and seal around its perimeter by poking in lengths of foam pipe insulation. Or buy one of the inflatable vinyl balloons made for the purpose. They are available in both square and round shapes. Choose one to fit your flue. Clean the flue, check it for sharp projections that might pop the balloon, insert the balloon, and then blow it up to make an airtight plug. While you're at it, attach a note to the fireplace or woodstove to alert anyone about to start a fire that the plug is in place.

If you long for a fire on winter evenings, install a direct-vent (sealed-combustion) gas fireplace. They don't draw air from your home—and they can put about 70 percent of the heat they generate back into the room.

3

REPLACING WINDOWS AND DOORS

A completely energy-efficient house would look like no home you know. There would be no windows—the heat lost through windows alone costs this country 2 million barrels of oil a day in lost energy. Taken together, doors and windows account for about one-third of a home's heat loss, so the door—there would have to be a door—would be a highly insulated plug.

But leaking doors and windows, by and large, are the doors and windows of days gone by. Today's windows insulate nearly 4 times as well as the best products on the market just 20 years ago—new high-performance windows can block the cold as well as an insulated wall. With new windows and doors, rooms that were cold in the winter can now be comfortable without having the thermostat turned up. And if energy-efficient windows get direct sunlight, they can even be a net supplier of heat.

But this is not a pitch to run out and replace every window in your home. It can take years for the energy savings to offset the cost, and if your windows are weather stripped and in reasonably good shape, it may be cheaper to live with the windows you have. Obviously, if a window is beyond the point where it can be patched and painted into reasonable shape, a new window is the ticket to both the repair and reducing your heating and cooling costs. And if you are adding on or renovating your home, it makes sense to get the most energy-efficient windows that you can afford.

WINDOWS ON THE WORLD

Energy-efficient windows come in all sizes and shapes—traditional double-hung, sliding, casement, hopper, awning, and bay. (A hopper window is a casement window with the hinge in the bottom; an awning window has the hinge on top.) Casement awnings, and hoppers can seal out air

Some Windows Are Leakier than Others

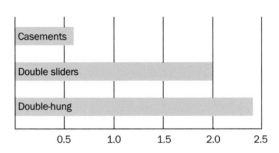

Air leakage in cubic feet per minute per foot of seam

Source: Lawrence Berkeley Labs

Air leakage rates vary greatly among windows from different manfacturers; but in general, some types leak more than others. Double-hung windows leak the most. Casement windows, which have fewer moving parts, leak the least. Sliding windows fall in between.

" Energy-efficient windows come in all sizes and shapes—traditional double-hung, sliding, casement, hopper, awning, and bay. "

leaks better than double-hung windows because these hinged windows compress their weather seals when closed. Also, when opened, hinged windows make the entire window opening available to capture summer breezes, while double-hung windows expose only half the opening.

Early windows were divided into smaller panes by strips known as muntins, because it was very hard to produce large sheets of glass. Today, many people still like the traditional look of smaller panes. Though you still can buy windows with true divided lights (or individual panes) held within muntins, a more popular and more affordable option is to use a larger-pane window and add a grid that looks like muntins. The grid may be placed permanently between double panes, or it may snap in place from inside the

■ ■ Window Aid

Check with your public utility to see whether it offers incentives to homeowners who install energy-efficient windows. Utilities sometimes offer partial reimbursement or low- or no-interest loans to help pay for energy-efficient improvements.

" Buying and installing new windows can lower your heating and cooling bills and upgrade the appearance of your house. But the expense is considerable."

Repair or Replace?

Windows tend to take a beating—from the weather and from being opened and closed countless times. If you have old windows, you may need to decide whether to repair your current windows or shop for new ones. Buying and installing new windows can lower your heating and cooling bills and upgrade the appearance of your house. But the expense is considerable, and you'll want to evaluate the benefits before committing yourself. You can usually make existing windows far more energy-efficient simply by weather stripping and adding storm windows.

Start by caulking and weather stripping the window as explained in Chapter 2, Plugging the

This window is clearly beyond repair. Replacing it would make the house warmer and would be an investment instead of a patch job. If, however, you live in a historic house—a Victorian, an Arts and Crafts bungalow, or a 100-year-old farmhouse—replacing windows can lower the value of the house. A repair covered by a good storm window may be the answer.

home. These windows cost less to produce than those with true divided lights, they're easier to keep clean, and they're even somewhat more energy-efficient.

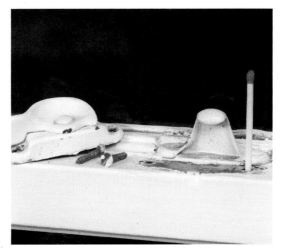

Sash locks do more than keep out burglars. They pull the sashes together, helping to seal out drafts. If your sash lock has worked loose, remove it. Put a drop of glue on a few wooden matchsticks and put the matchsticks in the screw holes. When the glue has dried, break the matchsticks off, drill a hole slightly smaller than the diameter of each screw, and drive the screws into the new holes.

If your windows are painted shut, cut through the paint with a sash saw. Put the saw teeth along the seam that the paint has sealed, and slide it along the window. One pass per seam is usually all it takes to free the window.

" The single pane of glass in older windows offers little insulation from outdoor temperatures. "

Leaks. Then, if your windows are wooden, turn your attention to the lock. It's there to prevent people from climbing in, of course. But the lock also serves to bring the two sashes tightly together to seal out the weather. If the lock is loose, you may have to remove it and plug the screw holes with wood glue and wooden matchsticks. Dip the plain end of a wooden matchstick in glue and push it snugly into the hole. Once the patch-up has dried fully, you can break off the match, drill pilot holes for the screws, and drive them back in.

If the sashes stick, you can make the channels in which they slide a little more slippery. A trusty old-time method is to rub all three sides of each channel with the bottom end of a white candle or a bit of paste wax. Silicone spray also will work, but it's more difficult to control, and the affected surfaces will repel paint.

Older windows are often painted shut. This may give you a nice, weathertight seal in the win-ter, and you might choose to leave the upper sash painted shut. But you'll surely want to free bottom sashes so you can capture cool night breezes in the summer. Cut away the paint with a sash saw, available at hardware stores and home centers.

The single pane of glass in older windows offers little insulation from outdoor temperatures. The traditional way of bumping up the energy efficiency of a window was to put shutters over it. Then along came the storm window, a relatively inexpensive but clumsy way of creating an insulat-ing layer of air between two panes of glass. If you

> *For best performance, choose storms with a low-E coating.*

have single-pane windows that are draining heat from the house, you can add new storms for about one-third the price of replacing them with new energy-efficient units. The payback period for storm windows typically runs between 5 and 10 years. Or, if you already have storm windows and they are cracked, loose-fitting, or even inoperable, it may make sense to replace them.

For best performance, choose storms with a low-E (low-emissivity) coating. The most readily available storms are triple-track storm windows. The frame screws in place over your window. Two half storms and a half screen slide up and down in tracks in the frame, and you can arrange them to create a single storm, or a window that is half storm and half screen. You can also take the screen and storms out of their tracks so that you can clean them and the window they cover.

If you have traditional wood-framed storms that you hang every fall and remove every spring, they're probably good storms, even if they are somewhat inconvenient. A good-quality wooden window, covered by a traditional storm window, approaches the thermal efficiency of a modern double-glazed window and surpasses the efficiency of some older double-glazed windows.

Interior storm windows are another possibility. Interior storms attach to the window jambs in a variety of ways—often with a simple turnbuckle, and often via a low-profile frame that attaches to the

window. Because the seal can be much tighter than on exterior storms, interior storms are often more effective than exterior storms. You must, however, make sure that whatever system you are using seals tightly. Leaks not only reduce the efficiency of the storm, they can let in moisture, which condenses and can damage a wood-framed window.

Gas, Glass, and Low-E Coatings

Storm windows are less common these days because double- and even triple-pane windows

Caulk along the edges of a storm window to keep air and water from leaking in. Do not cover the small holes in the bottom of the frame, however. They let trapped moisture filter out so that it doesn't rot the wood. If the house siding is wood, also caulk where the siding butts into the window casing.

have become standard. Multiple-pane windows are a lot more convenient and more attractive than storm windows.

The theory behind multiple-pane windows is that the more layers of glass you put in a given window, the more energy-efficient it will be. But going to three or even four panes won't yield dramatic savings—they are heavier, cost more, and can noticeably block visible light. Instead of layers of glass, high-performance windows

" Double-pane, gas-filled, low-E windows can outperform the triple-glazed units that once set the standard. "

combine a special low-E coating with an insulating gas between the panes. The gases—air, krypton, and argon—slow the passage of heat through the window, with krypton per-

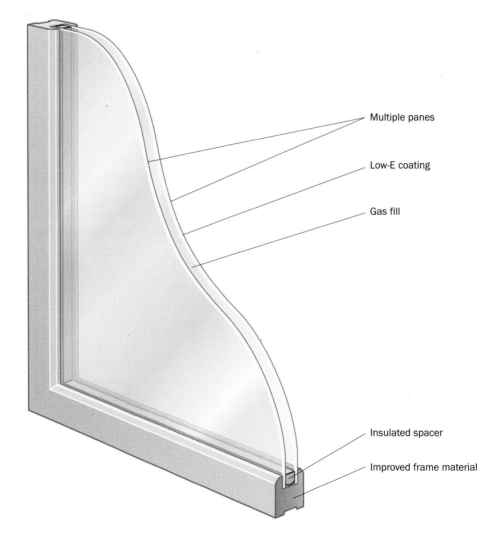

Multiple panes

Low-E coating

Gas fill

Insulated spacer

Improved frame material

A double-pane window can be as energy-efficient as a solid wall. Two layers of glass double the amount of insulation provided by a single-pane window. Argon or krypton gas between the panes further reduces heat loss. The low-E coating can either keep out solar heat or let it in, depending on the window you buy.

forming marginally better at a slightly higher cost. Double-pane, gas-filled, low-E windows can outperform the triple-glazed units that once set the standard. (Triple glazing remains valuable where winters are severe; in Manitoba, Canada, for example, three-pane low-E windows are the norm in new construction.)

The Energy Alphabet Game

When it comes to describing just how well or poorly a window or door performs, it's not enough to talk in terms of warm and cold. There are a few abbreviations you should become familiar with.

- **R-value** is a measure of a product's resistance to heat transfer. The higher the R-value, the better a material is at resisting heat loss (or gain).

- The **U-factor** measures the rate of heat transfer, and is the rating most commonly used for windows. It's the inverse of the R-value, making it equal to 1 divided by R. More simply, the lower the U-factor, the more something blocks the transfer of energy.

- The **Solar Heat Gain Coefficient,** or SHGC, is a measure of the amount of solar energy a window transmits. A high number means that more sunlight (and warmth) will be admitted.

While you're dealing with numbers, you should also consider the rate at which windows leak air, expressed in terms of cubic feet leaked per minute per foot of seam (cfm/ft). The higher the number, the greater the draft you'll be sitting near. For casement and awning windows, look for a window that leaks at most 0.1 cfm/ft. Because double-hung and slider windows tend to not be as tight, shoot for 0.2 or lower with them. Storm windows ideally will have a rating as low as 0.01 cfm/ft; try not to go above

0.3 cfm/ft. Most of the windows that CONSUMER REPORTS tested did a very good or excellent job at sealing out a fairly strong wind when the outside thermometer registered a mild 70° F. But when the temperature dropped to zero, only a handful performed well because weather stripping and other sealing components tend to stiffen or shrink.

A Window-Selection Tool

It can be daunting to sort through the many options offered by window manufacturers, all the more so because the best window for one part of the country may be a poor choice in another region. To simplify matters, use the window-selection tool at *www.ConsumerReports.org/energy* (click on Window Selection).

Enter the name of the nearest large city, then the type of glass and frame you are looking for, and the site gives you the annual energy costs of both heating and cooling for the window you have in mind. Once you've identified a window that meets your needs, the site suggests manufacturers that stock a model with those specifications.

For example, let's say you live near Philadelphia and are interested in a double-glazed window with a low-solar-gain low-E coating, with argon or krypton gas, and with an insulated vinyl or fiberglass frame. The site will tell you that with that kind of window, you might expect to spend $1,770 for heat and $85 for cooling. (Those figures are based on a 2,000-square-foot house with 300 square feet of window area.) Another click, and you've got the names of two manufacturers that can supply you with that type of window.

ConsumerReports.org/energy

Now that you understand the terminology, you can take a closer look at low-E glass. The coating on low-E glass is a thin film of metal or metallic oxide that keeps much of the home's heat inside in winter and bounces back a good portion of the summer sun. The coating can be manipulated to meet the needs of almost any area.

In northern areas with cool summers and cold winters, the best choice is an insulated glass window, which allows high solar gain to make the most of the sun's warming energy in winter months. A low U-factor will help to retain the home's heat. Many models that include argon gas and a low-E coating are available for about the same price as a standard insulated glass model.

In the north/central region, with its moderately hot summers and cold winters, look for windows with a low-E coating and argon or krypton that will screen solar heat somewhat in summer while insulating in winter.

The south/central region is characterized by hot summers and winters that may be either mild or cold. Windows should have a low-E coating to screen most of the sun's energy.

For southern areas, with their very hot summers, a window with two low-E coatings will reflect solar rays and reduce cooling costs by 40 percent or more. The glazing also blocks the UV rays that

Look for the Energy Star

Instead of trying to remember which kind of window to use where, you can just check for the Energy Star label.

The Energy Star program is run by the Department of Energy and labels products that save energy and help reduce greenhouse gases. When it comes to windows, the program has set standards for each part of the country. Energy Star-approved windows will have a map on the label telling you what part of the country the window is suited for.

Energy Star Criteria for Windows		
Energy Star Climate Zone	U-Factor	Solar Heat Gain Coefficient (SHGC)
Northern	0.35 or less	Any
North/North Central	0.40 or less	0.40 or less
South/Central	0.40 or less	0.40 or less
Southern	0.65 or less	0.40 or less

Clearly Quieter

By adding a second or third pane, you insulate the house from sound, too. The barrier that keeps your inside air from leaking out also helps keep outside noise from leaking in.

Window Performance			
Window type	R-value	U-factor	SHGC
Triple glazing with 2 low-E coatings, argon gas, insulated vinyl frame	6.2	0.15	0.37
Double glazing with a low-E coating, argon gas, wood or vinyl frame	3.0-3.3	0.33-0.30	0.55-0.44
Double glazing, wood or vinyl frame	2.0	0.49	0.58
Single glazing, aluminum frame, no thermal break	0.77	1.30	0.79
Single glazing, vinyl or wood frame	1.12	0.89	0.79

Source: U.S. Environmental Protection Agency

Tax Credits

The federal government recently passed a tax credit for installing energy-efficient windows and exterior doors. For more information, go to *www.ConsumerReports.org/energy* and click on Window and Door Tax Credits.

ConsumerReports.org/energy

cause curtains, upholstery, and carpets to fade, without interfering with the visible part of the spectrum. A gas fill of krypton or argon will insulate the home from extreme outdoor temperatures.

Skylights

Low-E coatings are especially important for skylights, whether you're considering adding or replacing them. Their orientation to the sun and location high in a room may mean that uncoated skylights bring in unwanted solar heat in the summer and lose a significant amount of heat in the winter.

The Frame Counts, Too

Energy Star Criteria for Skylights		
Energy Star Climate Zone	U-Factor	SHG Coefficient
Northern	0.60 or less	Any
North/Central	0.60 or less	0.40 or less
South/Central	0.60 or less	0.40 or less
Southern	0.75 or less	0.40 or less

E-Rated Films

If your windows don't have a low-E coating, you can buy low-E film and place it on the glass for far less than the cost of replacing the units. A good-quality film may remain effective for 10 to 15 years. The films can be most effective in hot climates, where the tinting helps reduce solar gain.

As high-tech as the glazing may be, the frame also plays a big part in a window's energy efficiency. Here is a rundown of frame materials.

■ **Wood** has the appearance that other materials try to match, but along with its traditional appeal comes the traditional chore of painting. Without regular attention, wooden windows are vulnerable to rot and weathering. Some manufacturers address this by covering the exterior of wooden sashes and frames with vinyl or aluminum. Wood is more expensive than other materials.

■ **Vinyl** windows have become the most popular choice, in part because inexpensive lines are available. On the other hand, several vinyl units were among the lower-performing windows tested by CONSUMER REPORTS. On the plus side, vinyl is relatively impervious to moisture and doesn't need to be painted. Vinyl windows with an insulated core offer very good thermal resistance. At extremely low temperatures, vinyl may be prone to cracking.

■ **Aluminum** is strong and durable, but it is an excellent conductor of heat and readily radiates it into or out of the house. As a result, the area around the windows is apt to feel chilly when it's cold outside and warm when it's hot outside. Condensed moisture or even frost may appear on the inside of the frame in cold weather. High-performance aluminum windows remedy those shortcomings with a thermal break between interior and exterior parts of the frame.

■ **Fiberglass** frames are less common. They are rugged and resist rot and warping, but they must be protected with paint. Some frames are hollow, but you can also get more energy-efficient frames with voids that have been filled with insulation.

■ A new wrinkle in frame materials is a **composite** made from wood and polymers. Rotting is less of a problem than with wood, and the frames will accept paint or stain. There's an advantage for the environment, too: The frames are made in part from recycled wood scraps and sawdust.

To see how different windows would affect costs in a northern and a southern city, see the chart "Window Costs Compared," below.

The Bottom Line

Low-E coatings do save a significant amount of energy over the life of the window, but it's probably not worth spending more than 10 to 20 percent of the cost of the window to get it. Fortunately, low-E coating has become standard as a no-added-cost feature in many windows. Whatever choice you make, look for the Energy Star label on windows, certifying that they have met criteria established by the Department of Energy and the EPA. Depending on the manufacturer, you also may see the label for the National Fenestration Rating Council (NFRC). This independent organization tests and certifies windows, doors, and skylights and gives ratings for U-factor, SHGC (Solar Heat Gain Coefficient), clarity of the glass, air leakage, and the resistance to condensation on the interior surface.

■ ■ Water on the Window

When moist, warm air from the house hits a cold windowpane, the moisture condenses and runs down the glass. A high-efficiency window has less condensation because the temperature of the inner glass pane is relatively close to that of the room. On humid mornings following cool nights, there may be a mist of condensed dew on the window. If there is condensation between the panes, however, the seal that traps the gas is broken and the window needs to be repaired before it begins to rot.

> " Low-E coating has become standard as a no-cost-added feature in many windows. "

■ ■ Daylighting

Energy-efficient windows tend to make rooms brighter, as well as more comfortable. Their coatings allow you to take better advantage of sunlight without closing the curtains to block out summer heat or keep in winter warmth. You'll also be less likely to turn on the lights, which is another way these windows can reduce utility bills.

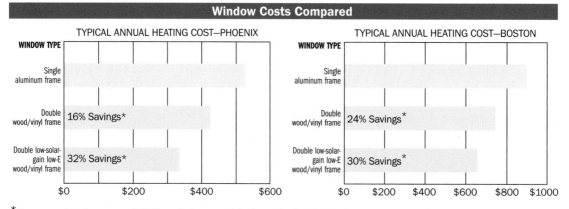

Window Costs Compared

TYPICAL ANNUAL HEATING COST—PHOENIX

WINDOW TYPE	
Single aluminum frame	
Double wood/vinyl frame	16% Savings*
Double low-solar-gain low-E wood/vinyl frame	32% Savings*

$0 $200 $400 $600

TYPICAL ANNUAL HEATING COST—BOSTON

WINDOW TYPE	
Single aluminum frame	
Double wood/vinyl frame	24% Savings*
Double low-solar-gain low-E wood/vinyl frame	30% Savings*

$0 $200 $400 $600 $800 $1000

*Compared to the same 2,000 sq.ft. house with clear single glazing in an aluminum frame.

ENERGY-EFFICIENT DOORS

When it comes to energy efficiency, insulated steel and fiberglass doors have more insulating value than wooden doors, but if the doors include glass panels, the differences really don't matter much. You are likely to save more money by stopping air leaks around the door than by replacing wood with fiberglass or steel. If your current door leaves you feeling cold, first check to see whether it's weather stripped, and if so, whether the weather stripping is intact. Then check to make sure the weather stripping is doing its job. Among other things, you can look for light leaking in around the edges of the door, or you can pass your hand along the perimeter of the door on a windy day to feel for drafts where the weather stripping may not seal properly. For more on weather stripping, see Chapter 2, Plugging the Leaks.

You might think seriously about replacing an older door if it is structurally weak and rotted, or if it has warped so badly that no reasonable amount of weather stripping can create a good seal within the frame. On the other hand, don't be in a rush to jettison a door that still is attractive and needs only a bit of attention. Try these simple tune-ups first.

■ If the door squeaks like something on the set of a horror movie, try putting some dry lubricant on each hinge as you move the door back and forth.

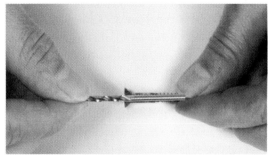

If a screw turns without tightening, it is loose in its hole and may cause the door to sag. Try using a longer screw that will bite into the stud. If that doesn't work, fill the hole with a dowel, and then drill the proper sized hole in the dowel. Start by putting the dowel in the hole, marking it, and cutting it about $1/8$ inch short of the mark (top). Glue the dowel in place by brushing glue over it before you put it back in the hole. When the glue dries, drill a hole for the screw that is the size of the screw shank, minus the width of the threads (middle). Drive the original screw in the new hole and tighten (bottom).

Longer screws driven through the jamb at the upper hinge plate into the wall stud can help a sagging door. Replacing the hinges or shimming out the lower hinge with one or more thicknesses of playing cards can also help.

■ A door that sticks when closed may need to be sanded or planed until it swings freely. Look for worn spots to identify where you need to remove a bit of wood.

■ Over time, one side of the door frame may have settled slightly lower than the other side, leaving the opening slightly out of square. Check to see whether the gap along the top of the door is uniform. If the gap is noticeably larger on the hinge side, cut a playing card to fit and place it in the top hinge pocket. If the gap is noticeably larger on the latch side, put the card in the bottom pocket.

■ Rattling knobs and flimsy locks may be irritating, but you can buy top-of-the-line replacements for a fraction of the price of a new door.

■ If the door is hanging loosely from its hinges, and tightening the screws doesn't help, try driving in longer screws to secure to the stud. If that doesn't work, then plug the holes with dowels and glue, drill holes slightly narrower than the screws, and reinsert the existing screws.

Shopping for a New Door

If you decide to go looking for a new door, you'll find that insulated models can be an improvement—in performance, if not necessarily in appearance. A steel or fiberglass door with a polyurethane core and no glass insert can have an R-factor of up to three times that of a solid-wood door. All new doors should be well weather stripped, but check to see whether the bottom edge is well sealed by an adjustable threshold or a sweep. Note that a window in a door can substantially lower the door's overall insulation value, depending on the rating for the glazing itself.

Fiberglass is weather-resistant and can be made to resemble wood—some doors will even take a

> *" A steel or fiberglass door with a polyurethane core and no glass insert can have an R-factor of up to three times that of a solid-wood door. "*

Comparing Doors

For a comparison of entry doors made of fiberglass, steel, and wood, go to *www.ConsumerReports.org/energy* and click on Door Ratings. The doors tested vary considerably in terms of cost, durability, and appearance, though no one door was head-and-shoulders above the others.

ConsumerReports.org/energy

---

stained finish. Fiberglass doors are a very practical choice for most applications. Expect to pay from $300 to $1,750 for a fiberglass door.

Metal doors, at their plainest, look like a flat slab, but you can find models formed to mimic most conventional door styles. You also are limited to the number of colors offered by the manufacturer, but the doors can be painted. CONSUMER REPORTS tests show that a $135 steel front door can be the equal of one in fiberglass or solid wood costing up to five times as much. Steel doors may be vulnerable to rust and dents; over time, you can expect them to look more beat up than those made of fiberglass or wood. Prices range up from a little more than $100 to the neighborhood of $1,500.

Wood remains the standard, in terms of appearance. As with windows, wooden exterior doors will need painting or varnishing over the years to ensure their durability. Given frequent attention, they should show less wear and tear than fiberglass and metal doors. Although most wooden entry doors are solid and have limited insulation value, you can custom-order foam-core wooden doors that are essentially two thin doors put together over a foam core. There's a great range of options to be had from specialty firms, with prices beginning around $500 and soaring to well above $2,500.

Patio Doors

As with windows, glass patio doors benefit from having a low-E coating and low-conductivity gas between multiple panes. If you have single-glazed sliding doors, or double-glazed sliders that are leaky around the edges, you've got a good candidate

If you're buying or replacing patio doors, hinged doors like these have a better long-distance track record. The weather stripping holds up well on hinged doors; the gaskets on sliding doors often fail over time.

for replacement or repair. Consider replacing them with a hinged door with high-performance glazing. Sliding doors that have become drafty should have their weatherstripping replaced. If the door or frame is damaged or rotted, consider replacement. Window coverings such as insulated drapes can block much of the cold radiating through the glass.

What about Storm Doors?

According to the Department of Housing and Urban Development, a new storm door may have a reasonable payback period if it costs no more than $200 and is used over an older door, particularly if the door is prone to leaks. A storm door also will help preserve a handsome wooden front door, and it presents another potential level of security when locked. But the investment isn't as likely to make good economic sense if you've got a fairly new foam-core door.

Some metal storm doors have an insulated core and double-pane glazing, making them all the more effective. Note that there is a potential for trouble if a storm door with a lot of glass creates a mini-greenhouse; the trapped air may be heated to the point that the entry door is damaged. Use a storm door that is only half glazed if the doorway receives more than a few hours of direct sunlight per day.

" A new storm door may have a reasonable payback period if it costs no more than $200 and is used over an older door. "

Storm doors can save you money if used over older wooden doors like this one, and if the storm isn't too expensive. If the door receives more than a few hours of direct sunlight, get a door that is only half glass so that the heat generated doesn't damage the entry door.

4

INSULATION AND VENTILATION

54

Once you've plugged the leaks in your home (and you know the drill if you've read Chapter 2), you're ready to insulate it. Insulating a house is easiest when it's being built and the studs and joists are still exposed; but even if your home was finished decades ago, there is still a lot you can do to make it more comfortable. Not only can you upgrade the insulation, you should: Recommended insulation levels have increased over the years, and the older your house, the more likely that the insulation that once was considered adequate is now considered substandard. According to the U.S. Department of Energy, only 20 percent of homes built before 1980 can be considered well-insulated.

ASSESSING YOUR INSULATION NEEDS

The first step is to find out what insulation your home currently has. This is straightforward in some parts of the house—an unfinished attic, for example—where the fiberglass batts or loose fill or foam is in plain sight. It takes more detective work to determine what, if anything, is inside the finished walls. You can have a private firm or a utility do a home energy audit and then recommend where your dollars would best be spent. For more information, see "Finding the Leaks," page 8. Or, you can do the inspection yourself, going around the home with a clipboard, a flashlight, and a spirit of exploration. As you peek and prod, one of the things you're going to look into is the R-value of whatever insulation you have.

Insulating a house is easiest when it's being built and the studs and joists are still exposed; but even if your home was finished decades ago, there is still a lot you can do to make it more comfortable.

Obviously, people living in extreme climates need greater R-values than those in moderate climates. You will also need a greater R-value in some parts of the house than in others.

R-value is the resistance of a material to the transfer of heat. Technically, R-value is determined by measuring energy requirements and temperatures on both sides of a wall, floor, or ceiling for a period of time, calculating the energy lost and the time it took. Practically speaking, the higher the R-value, the better the insulation.

How much R-value is enough? Obviously, people living in extreme climates such as Alaska and southern Florida need greater R-values than those in moderate climates such as Maryland. You will also need a greater R-value in some parts of

---

ZIP-Code Insulation Calculator

For a quick guide to how much it would cost to bulk up the R-value of various parts of your home, go to *www.ConsumerReports.org/energy* and click on ZIP-Code Insulation Calculator to visit the Department of Energy's ZIP code site. Once you're there, plug in the first three digits of your postal code, then go on to enter details about your house. The site recommends the most cost-efficient level of insulation for your house, then tells you what it might cost.

For example, you might find that to bring an uninsulated attic up to a level of R-38, you could expect to pay 67 cents per square foot, including both materials and labor. Unfortunately, the calculator does not include calculations for brick or stone houses or for homeowners who heat with wood or coal.

ConsumerReports.org/energy

How Much Insulation Do I Need?

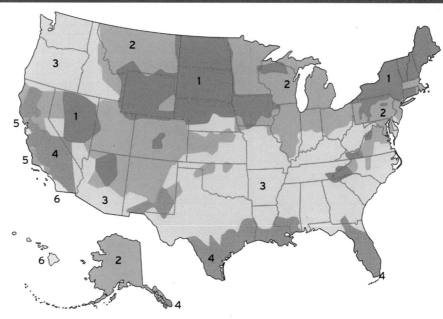

Find the area you live in on the map, and check the chart to see how much insulation you should have for a particular area of your house. Amounts are based on fuel costs and typical heating seasons rather than building codes. Double-check with the municipality you live in, and install whichever amount of insulation is greater.

Zone	Gas	Heat pump	Fuel oil	Electric furnace	Attic	Cathedral ceiling	Wall	Floor above base-ment	Crawl space*	Slab edge	Inside base-ment wall	Outside base-ment wall
1	√	√	√		R-49	R-38	R-18	R-25	R-19	R-8	R-11	R-10
1				√	R-49	R-60	R-28	R-25	R-19	R-8	R-19	R-15
2	√	√	√		R-49	R-38	R-18	R-25	R-19	R-8	R-11	R-10
2				√	R-49	R-38	R-22	R-25	R-19	R-8	R-19	R-15
3	√	√	√	√	R-49	R-38	R-18	R-25	R-19	R-8	R-11	R-10
4	√	√	√		R-38	R-38	R-13	R-13	R-19	R-4	R-11	R-4
4				√	R-49	R-38	R-18	R-25	R-19	R-8	R-11	R-10
5	√				R-38	R-30	R-13	R-11	R-13	R-4	R-11	R-4
5		√	√		R-38	R-38	R-13	R-13	R-19	R-4	R-11	R-4
5				√	R-49	R-38	R-18	R-25	R-19	R-8	R-11	R-10
6	√				R-22	R-22	R-11	R-11	R-11	**	R-11	R-4
6		√	√		R-38	R-30	R-13	R-11	R-13	R-4	R-11	R-4
6				√	R-49	R-38	R-18	R-25	R-19	R-8	R-11	R-10

* Insulate crawl space walls only if the space is dry, there is no insulation in the floor above, and all ventilation to the space is blocked.

** Not recommended.

	Insulation Checklist					
Location	Insulated? Yes/No	Type	Thickness	R-value	Desired R-value	Insulation condition
Top of foundation						
Basement walls						
Basement ceiling						
Room walls						
Attic floor						
Attic soffits						
Roof						
Garage wall						
House wall						
Garage ceiling						
Crawl Space ceiling						

the house than in others: Your roof, which leaks a lot of heat, needs to be better insulated than your walls, which leak less. To determine the recommended R-values for your area, consult the map and chart on page 55. Enter the recommended R-values before you start your insulation inspection. Fill out the rest of the checklist as you go through the house.

Looking at the columns from left to right, a typical row might contain the following entries shown in italics. Yes, there was insulation. It was made of *fiberglass batts*. There seemed to be *3 inches* of it for an R-value of *8.7* (R=2.9×3"), according to

the insulation R-values chart on page 65. The recommended amount of insulation is *R-18*. (Numbers vary from area to area, so be sure to check the map and chart "How Much Insulation Do I Need," page 55, for the actual recommendation.) An entry like "water stains on west wall" would remind you to look for the source of the leak so that it doesn't damage either the framing or the insulation.

Inspecting the Basement

If all but the top couple of feet of your foundation is below ground, then the basement is already benefiting from the temperature of the surrounding soil, which is usually warmer than the air in the winter, and cooler in the summer. Still, the temperature in the basement is not likely to be as warm or cool as you'd like. If the basement is unheated, you can insulate the basement ceiling and leave the walls alone. If the basement is heated or you have plans to use the space as more than a utility area, the logical choice would be to insulate the walls. Either approach will reduce heat loss or gain by about the same amount.

Making up a Checklist

Having a checklist when you do your energy audit organizes the information so that you can evaluate the situation in a single glance. There's a copy of the checklist shown above at *www.ConsumerReports.org/energy*. Click on Insulation Checklist to download a copy.

ConsumerReports.org/energy

The table "Savings from Insulating Basement Walls," page 58, shows you how much you might save at two R-value levels in different parts of the U.S. The figures are based on a 1,500-square-foot house heated with natural gas.

Insulating the ceiling can be a hassle because of all the wires, pipes, and ducts that you're apt to see snaking along there. But if the basement isn't heated, you may want to place insulation between it and the rooms above. Be aware that this could make the basement cooler and that water pipes there may be more vulnerable to freezing; you may need to wrap pipes with heat tape. Warm-air ducts should be insulated, as explained in "Sealing Ductwork," page 36.

Walls tell you a lot about your basement. A basement like this, with solid concrete walls, probably has foam insulation against the outside of the wall. If the wall is room temperature when you put your hand against it in the winter, there's no need for additional insulation either between the floors or against the wall. Some concrete walls, and most concrete block, brick, or stone walls, will feel cold, however. If so, the basement is a candidate for more insulation. You can finish the basement walls with drywall and insulation or insulate the ceiling to keep the household heat from escaping into an unoccupied space.

Inspecting Rooms

It's a challenge to know what's inside your walls, but it's not impossible. The cutouts for outlets and switches are always slightly bigger than the outlets and switches themselves. This provides a very small window into the wall, but one big enough to find out what you need to know.

Find an outlet on an exterior wall, and turn off the circuit breaker or unscrew the fuse that powers it. Test to make sure the power is off by plugging a lamp or radio into the outlet. When you're sure the power is off, remove the cover plate and insert a thin wooden ruler through the insulation until it touches the outside wall. If the ruler goes all the way to the exterior wall with no resistance, there is no insulation

Savings from Insulating Basement Walls		
City	R-10	R-20
Buffalo	$350	$390
Denver	310	360
Minneapolis	400	450
Seattle	280	320
St. Louis	250	290
Washington, DC	250	280

Note: Annual savings shown are based on a 1,500-square-foot basement, using either R-10 or R-20 insulation, and natural gas priced at $7.20 per 1,000 cubic feet.

> " *It's a challenge to know what's inside your walls, but it's not impossible.* "

in the wall, and it is a candidate for some sort of blown-in insulation. (If there is insulation, it will interfere with blowing in more insulation, whether or not the existing insulation is adequate. See "Frame Walls," page 67, for possible solutions.)

■ ■ ■ Insulating Crawl Spaces and Garage Ceilings

Instead of a basement, many homes have a crawl space beneath them. To insulate a crawl space, put insulation between the floor joists, as if you were insulating a basement. (See "Insulating a Basement Ceiling," page 70.) The vapor barrier should face the heated space in the North, and be placed as described in "Vapor Barriers," page 62, in the South. When you're done insulating, cover the dirt floor with 4- to 6-mil plastic to keep humidity in the ground from working its way into the insulation.

If your garage has a ceiling that has a heated space above it, insulate it like you would a basement ceiling, positioning the vapor barrier as required in your area—unlike a crawl space, no vapor barrier is required on the attic floor. You should, however, seal the joint between the top sill and the header the same way you seal the joint between the basement sill plate and the rim joist, as explained in "Down in the Basement," page 9.

Outlets are a window into the wall. Turn off the power and probe with a wooden ruler to see how much insulation there is inside the wall.

Inspecting the Attic

When you review the home's insulation, the attic deserves particular attention. Because warm air rises, this uppermost part of the house is prone to losing the most heat. And because the roof takes the full brunt of the sun, overheating can also be a problem in the summer. Keep an eye out for moisture, stains, mold, and rotting wood, too—all are signs of a leaky roof. Make any necessary repairs to roofing and flashing, and then weather strip and caulk before insulating.

Attics can be insulated in one of two places: the floor or the ceiling. If the insulation is fiberglass, roll back a batt to see how thick it is. (If the fiberglass batts have a facing, the R-value is usually printed on it.) If the insulation is loose-fill, put a ruler through it to measure its thickness; lift up foam boards to measure their thickness.

If you have finished knee walls—low walls that parallel the eaves—check them for insulation. (This applies to finished knee walls only; don't worry about any unfinished walls in the attic.)

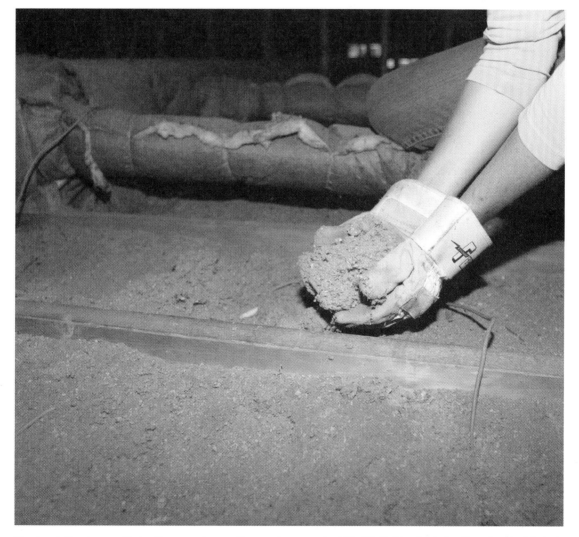

The insulation in an attic is often easy to see if you poke around a little bit. Rolling back the fiberglass in this attic revealed a layer of cellulose.

If there's no entry hatch in the wall, you may have to cut one in order to look behind the wall. You can make a temporary hole and then seal it, or create a permanent door so that you can use the space for storage. (If you're planning on a doorway, check at the home center for prefab hatches.)

DO IT YOURSELF?

You could save a substantial sum by insulating some or all of your home yourself, but first consider whether you really want to. When insulating, you are going to find yourself in the darkest, the dampest, and the hottest nooks and crannies of your home—less-than-pleasant spots that most homeowners seldom visit. Chances are you'll have to do some yogalike bending and stretching to place insulation where it has to go. Lighting will be poor. And you have to take precautions to protect your skin and lungs if you will be handling insulation.

Any surface covered by a wall, floor, or ceiling will be a special challenge. Either you will have to remove and replace the existing surface, or you will have to cut holes in it and blow in insulation. Be prepared to cut a hole in the top and bottom of your wall every 16 inches. Be prepared to patch those holes, too—a fussy process that seldom results in an invisible repair. Unless you're insulating only

Cellulose blows in easily and quickly and can insulate exterior walls as well as attic floors. It's versatile enough to insulate everything from an old house to the new school shown here.

" No single insulating material is best. Each type of insulation has its strong points and limitations, depending on the application. "

an attic or a basement ceiling, it's probably best to leave the job to the pros.

When you find a contractor, be ready to talk about two things: what you'll use, and how you'll use it. No single insulating material is best. Each type of insulation has its strong points and limitations, depending on the application. If you live in an old house in an extremely cold area, for example, there may not be room in the wall for enough fiberglass, whereas foam may do the job. If you're insulating an unfinished basement ceiling, it's pretty hard to install loose fill from below; fiberglass may be the answer here even if it isn't elsewhere.

A Free, Customized Energy Plan

A Web site called Home Energy Saver can recommend the best energy retrofits for your house—your very own house. That's possible because the site asks for details about your home and your life. The factors cover the age of your home, its size and shape, the current state of your insulation and weather stripping, the shading provided by trees, and even how many minutes per week you use your espresso maker. All of that information is crunched in an instant, and you are presented with a list of energy-efficient improvements, including tips on products, information sites, and even ways of paying for those energy improvements. To get to this site, go to *www.ConsumerReports.org/energy*, and click on the link A Customized Energy Plan.

ConsumerReports·org/energy

This building has two kinds of insulation—the yellow foam sheets on the exterior were chosen because they provide a good base for the stucco that will go over them. The section to the left will get siding. The sheathing there is covered by Tyvek, a product that seals out wind and rain while letting water vapor escape. Insulation comes from fiberglass batts inside the wall.

Vapor Barriers

When insulating your house, think of wet and dry as well as hot and cold. Moisture can penetrate the wall from inside the house (from showers, cooking, and potted plants) as well as from the weather outside.

When moisture does penetrate the wall, problems develop. The relatively warm moisture hits the colder wall and condenses. The water can makes fiberglass and loose-fill insulation collapse, mold and mildew are apt to flourish, wooden framing may rot; and adjacent painted surfaces will blister and peel no matter how well you scrape and sand before painting.

A vapor barrier is a layer of material or paint that slows the diffusion of the water vapor. Where you put it depends on where you live. In cooler parts of the country (not shown on this map), the barrier should face the inside of the heated space. In a thin east-to-west zone running from the Carolinas to Texas, homes will function better with no barrier whatsoever. And in the hot and humid Gulf Region and Florida, there should be either no barrier, or one against the outside wall surface.

Some building materials serve as vapor barriers, including rigid foam insulation and fiberglass batts backed with aluminum or paper. Polyethylene sheeting of various thicknesses is commonly used in colder climates. Ordinary household paint is an excellent vapor for the two southernmost bands of the map below. Household paints with a higher percentage of pigment (check the label) will do a better job of slowing moisture's creep, as will glossier paints, which contain more resin than flat paints. You also can buy paint specially formulated to retard moisture diffusion. Talk to your contractor about which you should be using, and where. If you're doing the job yourself, the map below shows you what you'll need to do.

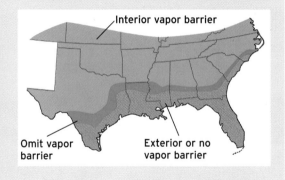

Fiberglass: R-Value 2.9 to 4.3

Fiberglass insulation is a popular choice—for accessible spaces. It is easy to handle and to install in most instances. You'll find it sold in rolls (referred to as blankets) or in precut batts of various thicknesses, with or without a paper moisture barrier. The precut batts are handy when you have lots of bays of a standard size to fill—8-foot-high walls, for example. For nonstandard lengths such as attic floors or ceilings, it makes more sense to cut rolls to length. (Some manufacturers make rolls and batts that are "encased"—wrapped in plastic—to contain the fibers and reduce itchy contact with them.)

Fiberglass batts have an R-value between 2.9 and 4.3.

■ ■ ■ Dressing for the Part

Fiberglass insulation looks something like cotton candy—a fluffy material that often comes in pretty pink. But the stuff can irritate your skin, and while there is no conclusive evidence that fiberglass is a health hazard, you certainly don't want to inhale any loose fibers. Consider using encased rolls or batts to further prevent itching. Here's your wardrobe, should you choose to take on an insulating assignment:

■ Long-sleeved shirt, with cuffs and collar buttoned

■ Long pants

■ Gloves

■ Dust mask specifically marked as being for fiberglass installation

■ Safety goggles

To avoid getting fiberglass fibers in the rest of the laundry, wear disposable coveralls (available at home centers and paint stores).

Fiberglass is also available as loose fill, to be poured or blown in by machine. If you choose to install fiberglass yourself, you will need to wear a dust mask because of the health hazards of breathing and touching the fibers. Wear safety glasses to protect your eyes and gloves to protect your hands.

There are several grades of fiberglass. Regular batts, which is what most older homes were built with, have an R-value of 2.9 to 3.8 per inch. High- and medium-density fiberglass batts have an R-value of 3.7 to 4.3 per inch.

You might be tempted to plump up a batt with the idea that it will have greater insulation value. But you can't coax a better R-value out of a batt. It's also counterproductive to cram fiberglass batts into a tight space. The insulation value depends on air trapped between the fibers, and you work against this when you compress the fiberglass. All that batts need is a quick shake, if anything, and then to be left alone while they gradually fluff up to full volume wherever you've installed them.

If ducts in the attic or basement run through fiberglass insulation, make sure the ducts themselves and the holes they travel through are well-sealed; otherwise, airborne particulates may be picked up and broadcast throughout the house.

Rigid Foam: R-Value 3.8 to 8.0

Lightweight sheets of rigid foam are made from one of three different plastics with varying R-values.

Polystyrene foam board, also known as "beadboard," is the same material that foam coffee cups are made of. It's made by heating polystyrene beads until they expand. The expanded beads are injected into a mold, where with more heat and pressure they expand further to become a sheet of insulation. Boards made this way are called "molded expanded polystyrene" or MEPS. Boards called extruded expanded polystyrene foam board and extruded polystyrene are similar to MEPS but are manufactured differently. All three have an R-value of 3.8 to 5 per inch. Polystyrene foam

Polyisocyanurate foam board (top) is faced with foil or plastic to trap in bubbles of gas that create the foam that gives it an R-value between 7 and 8 per inch. White polystyrene "bead board" is made of the same material as coffee cups and has an R-value between 3.8 and 5 per inch. Extruded polystyrene (bottom) is made of the same material but using a different manufacturing process; it also has an R-value of 3.8 to 5 per inch.

boards have no facing on them and are usually blue, pink, or yellow.

Polyurethane and polyisocyanurate foam have a higher R-value, typically between 7 and 8 per inch, and are manufactured via a chemical reaction. The reaction traps an insulating gas within the bubbles of foam. Over time, some of the gas would escape, causing the R-value to drop. Both foams, however, are faced with a foil that reflects heat back toward its source. The foil also keeps most of the insulating gas from escaping and keeps the R-value of the sheet fairly constant.

Because polyisocyanurates are dimensionally stable over a wide temperature range (−100° F to 250° F), they are often used when insulating roofs, and roofing sheets may be thicker.

While rigid foam sheets don't catch fire easily, they will burn and give off toxic gases. For this reason, they have to be covered on the inside of the home with drywall at least $1/2$ inch thick, or as required by local codes.

Loose Fill: R-Value 2.2 to 3.8

Loose fill may be fiberglass, cellulose, or rock wool. You can simply dump it from bags over an unfinished attic floor. To get it into a finished wall, however, usually requires specialized blowing equipment. Although it's possible to rent a blower and do this yourself, it's a job best left to professionals.

Cellulose is a recycled product made from newsprint and wood fiber. The newsprint and wood fiber are ground up and formed into fibers that will fill the smallest cavities. Cellulose is treated to make it fire- and insect-proof. It is not, however, waterproof—it will absorb and retain water that might come in through a leaky roof. Once installed, it will settle over time.

Loose-fill fiberglass insulation is much the same insulation you see in fiberglass batts. Instead of being in batt or blanket form, however, it comes in a bag of cotton ball–like puffs that the installer blows into wall, floor, or ceiling cavities. It's used in both new construction and retrofitting, and has an R-value somewhere between 2.2 and 2.7. Fiberglass loses 2 to 4 percent of its volume as it settles.

Like cellulose, rock wool is a recycled product, made from slag, a byproduct of steel manufacturing, or from naturally occurring rocks like basalt. The materials are heated to 2,500° F or higher, and become molten. The molten rock is poured over a spinning cylinder, which flings it off in fine strands that cool and become fibers.

Rock wool is waterproof, fireproof, and insect-proof and has an R-value of 3.0 to 3.3 per

Cellulose, made from recycled newspapers, has an R-value between 3.2 and 3.8 per inch.

Loose-fill fiberglass insulation has an R-value between 2.2 and 2.7.

Insulating Materials and Their R-Values		
Material	**Description**	**R-Value per Inch**
High-density fiberglass batts	Pink, yellow, or white blankets	3.7-4.3
Fiberglass batts	Pink, yellow, or white blankets	2.9-3.8
Loose-fill fiberglass	Pink, yellow, or white loose fibrous material	2.2-2.7
Loose-fill rock wool	Dense wooly material, usually gray with black specks (some newer products are white)	3.0-3.3
Loose-fill cellulose	Gray shredded newspaper	3.2-3.8
Expanded polystyrene board	Rigid plastic foam board	3.8-5.0
Extruded polystyrene board	Rigid plastic foam board	3.8-5.0
Polyisocyanurate board	Rigid plastic foam board	7.0-8.0
Polyurethane board	Rigid plastic foam board	7.0-8.0
Sprayed polyurethane foam	Plastic foam, uneven surface	6.5

Source: U.S. Department of Energy

inch. Rock wool loses 2 to 4 percent of its volume as it settles.

Blown-in loose fill will of course be out of sight, but you can make sure you're getting enough material by counting bags of insulation used. The contractor should use roughly one 30-pound bag of cellulose for every three spaces between studs, assuming they are 16 inches on center. (If your studs are 16 inches on center, and most are, the centers of the holes that the contractor drills will also be 16 inches apart.) If the contractor is installing fiberglass or rock wool, expect to use about 15 pounds of fiberglass or rock wool for every three wall cavities you fill.

Rock wool, made by heating rock until it's molten and then spinning it, has an R-value of 3.0 to 3.3.

Asbestos Alert

Loose-fill vermiculite insulation may contain naturally occurring asbestos, a fiber known to cause potentially serious health problems. While no longer used, vermiculite was a popular insulation from 1963 until 1984. If you find vermiculite in your home, do not try to remove it. Check the Yellow Pages under "Asbestos Consulting and Testing," or go to *www.ConsumerReports.org/ energy* and click on Dealing with Asbestos.

The job of removing vermiculite with asbestos should be entrusted to a certified firm.

Spray Foam: R-Value 6.5

Spray foam comes in several forms—including a cement-based foam—but the foam most commonly used in home insulation is polyurethane foam. With an R-value of 6.5 per inch of thickness, polyurethane foams are twice as effective as fiberglass batts, but appearances can be deceiving. Because the foam expands, it's easy to overfill the cavity with just enough foam to provide the required level of insulation. Where foam really shines is in its ability to seal air leaks. Foam expands to fill even the smallest cavities and then hardens to create an effective air barrier that further helps to block heat transmission.

Spray foam is most commonly used in new construction, before the drywall goes up. A technician sprays on a watery foam that sticks to the wall and expands up to 120 times its original size as it foams, hardens, and dries. There are some slow-rise, low-pressure expanding foams, however, which can be used for insulating existing homes. The low pressure reduces the chance of damaging the wall or door frame from over-expansion. Research the material that your contractor will use, and ask to speak to past customers before you agree to have the work done. You want to make sure the contractor was able to apply the insulation without doing damage. Even if a contractor is using slow-rise, low-pressure foam, it can do damage.

Foam Facts

For more information on all types of foam, go to *www.ConsumerReports.com/energy* and click on Foam Insulation.

ConsumerReports.org/energy

Spray foam has an R-value of 6.5 per inch. Because it expands after it's applied, installers avoid overfilling by stopping before there is enough foam to fill a space entirely. Foam clings tenaciously to whatever it touches, however, and provides an almost complete barrier against air infiltration.

WHERE TO INSULATE

You have three options for insulating exterior walls—on the outside, on the inside, or in the middle of the wall itself. Insulating inside the wall is the clear choice if remodeling gives you access. Otherwise, each of the three options presents its own challenges.

Frame Walls

If your home is frame construction, with studs in the wall, the cavity inside the wall can be filled with loose-fill insulation or with a low-pressure, slow-expanding foam. Getting the stuff in there usually involves having a contractor drill holes in the wall, either outside or inside the home. The contractor blows the insulation into walls, then patches the holes.

You can also apply insulation to the outside of the home: Place a layer of sheet foam right over the existing sheathing, or even over the old siding, and then install new siding. It's not quite as easy as it sounds: The insulation makes the walls thicker, leaving you with recessed windows, which at the very least will need special trim when the siding goes up. This is expensive, and another job best left to a contractor.

Older stud-wall houses may be constructed with a balloon framing system, in which studs run from the basement all the way to the roof without a break at each floor level. These open, chimney-like cavities are dangerous if a house catches fire, but they can make it easier to insulate. You can usually pour in loose insulation from the attic and have it run all the way down to the foundation.

Brick Walls

The brick walls on newer homes usually are a veneer over a conventional frame-wall insulation. If you're going to insulate, have insulation blown into the framed wall from inside the house.

> *You have three options for insulating exterior walls—on the outside, on the inside, or in the middle of the wall itself.*

If you have an older home with solid structural brick walls, there is no cavity to insulate. A contractor could insulate the exterior of brick walls by attaching furring strips to the brick and putting insulation between the strips, and then apply siding. But because brick is such a durable and handsome exterior surface, you are likely to rule out covering it up.

It's generally less expensive and easier to add the insulation to the inside of a brick wall. You can build out the walls with 2×4s or even 2×6s, put fiberglass batts between them, then put up drywall. It shrinks your room by the width of the stud, and it requires you to use wider jambs around windows and exterior doors. Alternatively, if you place $1\frac{1}{2}$-inch rigid foam boards between furring strips, you'll get roughly the same insulation value in half the space.

The Attic

You can expect to save up to 30 percent on your heating bills by insulating the floor of the attic. Even if the floor already has 6 or 7 inches of fiberglass, rock wool, or cellulose, you should probably consider adding more—the current standard for most of the U.S. is R-38, or 10 to 14 inches of insulation, depending on the material.

Attics can be confusing places to insulate, however. To begin with, the attic can be insulated in one of two places—between the floor joists or between the roof rafters. Roof-rafter insulation keeps heat or air-conditioned air inside the attic, so it's most commonly found in finished spaces such as an attic bedroom, the second floor of a Cape Cod home, or a cathedral ceiling of a modern home. Insulation between the rafters is different from insulation elsewhere in the house: Air needs to flow between the insulation and the roof sheathing to prevent damage caused by water condensation. This requires a vent in the soffit that lets air into the space above the insulation, and a vent in the roof ridge or at the top of the gable walls that lets the air back out. Installing these vents requires skill as well as the willingness to climb on your roof to cut a hole in it. If you're thinking about insulating a finished attic, this is reason enough to leave it to the pros.

Most attics, however, are unfinished and unheated, and if they have insulation, it should be between the floor joists.

If there's no floor in your attic, you can easily examine any insulation that might be there. Measure the thickness and find its R-value in the chart "Insulating Materials and Their R-Values," page 65. Then peel it back and look at both sides to see whether it has a vapor barrier. If there's a paper liner or a shiny liner that looks like aluminum foil, it's the vapor barrier. In colder climates the vapor barrier, if any, should face the heated part of the house; in warmer climates the vapor barrier should face the unheated section. Look at the map in "Vapor Barriers," page 62, to see where any vapor barrier ought to be in your home. You don't want a vapor barrier on both sides of the insulation because it could trap moisture and lead to loss of insulating value, mold, and wood decay.

What you've found in terms of insulation, vapor barrier, and existence of an attic floor determines how you insulate:

■ If there's a floor in your attic, it may be easy enough to take up the floor to insulate with fiberglass. Otherwise, the only way to insulate is to have insulation blown in. Talk to area contractors to see whether foam or cellulose insulation will work better.

> *Most attics are unfinished and unheated, and if they have insulation, it should be between the floor joists.*

■ If there's no floor and no insulation, you can either roll in fiberglass insulation or have insulation blown in. Check the chart "How Much Insulation Do I Need?", page 55, to find the required R-value.

■ If there's no floor and inadequate insulation, you can put in additional insulation, filling up the space between the joists and then rolling more insulation across the joists if necessary. If putting new insulation over old, always put in unfaced insulation so that it doesn't trap moisture between the new and old layers.

■ If there's no vapor barrier in an area that ought to have one, you can still add insulation. Make sure, however, that there's an open window or adequate vent space to let out moisture. You'll need at least 1 square foot of vent space for every 150 feet of attic floor.

■ If there is a vapor barrier in an area that requires vapor barriers, insulate over the existing insulation, using an unfaced insulation. Moisture may still slip through the vapor barrier: Make sure you have 1 square foot of vent space for every 300 square feet of attic floor.

■ If the vapor barrier appears to be facing the wrong way, check with your local building department to see what local practice is and whether the situation you face is likely to cause problems.

The Basement

If you have an unheated basement (or a crawl space, or a garage with rooms above), you not only can save energy by insulating, you can save money by doing it yourself. But the rules still hold—undertake the job only if the ceiling is unfinished. Pros can get insulation behind finished ceilings, and you're better off leaving it to them. Step-by-step directions follow, explaining how you can do the job—or what the contractor should do if you hire one.

Insulating the basement walls is a job best left to contractors, too. It requires framing out a wall, putting it next to the existing one, insulating the new wall, and then covering it with drywall. Don't have anyone insulate basement walls that weep moisture, or you'll risk creating a breeding ground for mold and mildew. Turn your attention outside first, and try to eliminate the source of the water. Often it's as simple as making sure the downspouts carry water away from the home. In other cases, you may need to raise the grade around the entire perimeter of the house so that all water flows away from the house. In extreme cases, you may need to dig around the home's foundation and install a drain that carries water elsewhere on the property. In any event, be sure to seal any cracks or holes around pipes, using caulk or expanding foam.

Even if you decide against insulating the basement walls or ceiling, have a look at one of the home's most notorious trouble spots: along the top of the foundation walls. The seams here should be sealed well; see "Down in the Basement," page 9. Once you've taken care of the leaks, add insulation to the top of the wall.

Insulate the space between the top of the foundation wall and the first floor to isolate the house from outside temperatures. Use the same R-value recommended for exterior walls, and cut it to manageable lengths. The insulation is often held in place by friction, but you can also use wire insulation supports, seen on page 71, to hold it in place.

Insulating a Basement Ceiling

Putting fiberglass batts on an unfinished ceiling is pretty straightforward. Make sure you are adequately protected with gloves, safety glasses, dust mask, and a long-sleeved shirt. If the shirt has buttons, button them all.

Insulating will do more than make your first floor warmer. It will also make the basement colder, as heat from upstairs no longer radiates into the space below. If you're using the basement for something like an occasional workshop or dark room, for example, you may need to rely on a space heater from time to time. If you have a heated basement for something like a rec room, insulating the basement ceiling will only keep basement heat from rising into your living space. Talk to a contrctor about having the walls insulated instead.

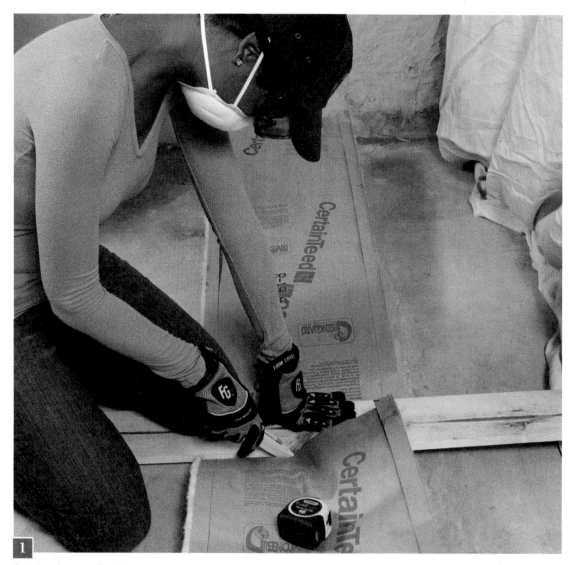

1

Cut the pieces to fit. Measure and cut the fiberglass to length. Cut with a utility knife guided along the edge of a board.

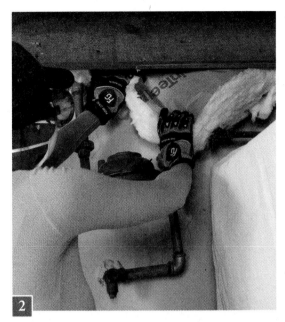

2

Install the batts. Insert fiberglass batts into the spaces between joists with the vapor barrier face up. Friction will hold the pieces temporarily in place.

3

Attach the batts. Attach the batts with insulation supports, which are pieces of springy wire, a bit longer than the space between joists. The supports flex into place between the joists.

4

Piece the insulation together around obstructions. You can tuck insulation between wires and the ceiling, but don't compress the insulation and lessen its R-value. Cut as necessary to fit around cross bracing, plumbing, and wiring that would compress the insulation. Butt the adjoining pieces together.

Insulating the Attic Floor

Even if your attic floor already has 6 or 7 inches of fiberglass, rock wool, or cellulose, you should probably consider adding more. The current standard for most of the U.S. is R-38, or 10 to 14 inches of insulation, depending on the material.

You can do the job yourself if there's no floor in the attic. If there is a floor, you may be able to rent a blower and blow insulation between the floor and the ceiling, though you may want to leave it to a pro. You could also lay insulation directly on top of the floor, though this, of course, means you can't store anything on top of it.

You're going to be working with fiberglass, which can severely irritate the skin, eyes, nasal passages, and anything else it comes into contact with, so take precautions. Wear goggles, a dust mask specifically labeled for fiberglass work, a hat, long sleeves, and long pants.

The fiberglass you use should be unfaced. This not only means the fiberglass is exposed on both sides, it means there's no vapor barrier. You don't need a vapor barrier if the existing insulation already has one. If there's no vapor barrier on the existing insulation—or no insulation at all—a properly built attic will have plenty of ventilation to carry out excess moisture.

Installing insulation against the roof is done most easily during construction, and care must be taken to provide adequate ventilation between the insulation and roof. In most cases, only cathedral ceilings and finished attics have insulated roofs. Insulating an attic floor is far simpler and is well within most homeowners' skills.

Put down planks. You'll need a place to sit, kneel, or stand as you work. Lay some planks or pieces of plywood across the joists, which are hidden here by insulation that was blown in when the house was built. Make sure you stand on the floor joists anytime you're not on the planks. Stepping directly on the ceiling will put a hole in it.

Install rafter vents. Install rafter vents to keep insulation away from the roof and to keep the vents in the soffit open. Start by moving any insulation away from the soffit vents. Put the rafter vent on the soffit, and staple it to the roof decking.

Cut vents to fit, if necessary. If the spacing between the rafters is narrow somewhere along the roof, you can cut a vent to fit. Most vents are perforated down the middle to make snapping them in half easier, and you can trim the flange to make an even narrower vent. Staple the vent in place.

Unroll the fiberglass batt. Start laying the insulation along the outside edges of the attic, and work toward the middle. If there is already insulation in place, lay the new insulation on top of it and perpendicular to the joists. If there's no insulation in place, put the insulation between the joists.

Cut the batt as needed. If you run into an obstruction, or if you reach the end of the attic before you reach the end of the fiberglass batt, cut it to fit. Make the cut with a utility knife, making several passes and guiding the knife against a straightedge.

Push the insulation in place. The slope of the roof gives you very little room to work on the first few pieces of insulation you install. Push the insulation into place with a piece of scrap wood.

Lay a second row of insulation. Keep laying insulation from the edge of the attic toward the center. Stop when you reach the center, and begin laying insulation along the edge you haven't insulated. Work your way from the edge to the center so that you won't have to walk across newly laid insulation.

Watch out for recessed lighting. Lighting that's recessed on one floor extends into the space between the joists on the next floor. When the lights extend into the attic, it can affect how you insulate. Some lights are designed so that you can insulate right up to them. If the lights are boxed in, like this one, the fixture gets too hot to come in contact with the insulation. Screw an extension to the box, and trim the insulation so it fits snugly against the extension.

5

ENERGY-EFFICIENT APPLIANCES

As energy prices climb, the efficiency of home appliances becomes increasingly important. Refrigerators, washing machines, dryers, dishwashers, and hot-water heaters—all are now being manufactured to perform better while using less electricity or gas. Beyond shopping with efficiency in mind, this chapter offers simple maintenance tips that will help coax the most out of your appliances. You'll also learn how to judge when it's best to replace aging appliances with state-of-the-art models.

REFRIGERATORS AND FREEZERS

Your refrigerator may only hum and gurgle pleasantly, but it's using a lot of watts to keep your food cold. There are a few strategies that you can follow to lower your electric bill.

> " *The coils release heat that the coolant has gathered from inside the unit. Layers of dust make this process more difficult and less efficient.* "

■ It's more cost-effective and energy-efficient to have one ample-sized refrigerator or freezer than two smaller units, so consolidate if possible.

■ Allow for some distance between the refrigerator or freezer and heat sources such as the oven, dishwasher, heat vents, and direct sunlight from a window.

■ Discourage family members from idly browsing the refrigerator shelves with the door wide open.

■ Keep the freezer full. Frozen food retains cold better than air does. This means that less cold will escape when you open a full freezer than one with less food in it.

■ Clean the coils. The coils release heat that the coolant has gathered from inside the unit. Layers of dust make this process more difficult and less efficient. (See "Refrigerator Maintenance," page 78.)

■ Set the thermostat for the refrigerator between 35° and 38° F. Set the freezer thermostat to 0°. If, like most models, your refrigerator doesn't have a temperature scale on the controls, use two appliance thermometers— one for the main compartment and one for the freezer.

Refrigerators with the freezer on either the top or the bottom will not only save you $5 to $20 a year in electricity costs compared with side-by-side models, they also generally have been more reliable.

Know When to Nix It

If the repair will cost more than half the price of a comparable new refrigerator, it is better to replace the unit.

Repair or Replace?

When is it time to pull the plug on an old icebox? Current Energy Star-qualified models are about 40 percent more efficient than conventional models built before 2001, and 50 percent more efficient than those from before 1993. A unit made before 1992 probably should be replaced if it needs service. Over its life, a new refrigerator will generally save enough energy to offset the purchase price. So even if you've been able to coax years of faithful service from a trusty refrigerator, you may be better off replacing it.

Energy Star-approved refrigerators use at least 15 percent less energy than current federal standards. They take advantage of high-efficiency compressors, improved insulation, and precise temperature and defrosting mechanisms. There's an environmental benefit, too: Compared with a 10-year-old fridge, a new Energy Star model saves enough electricity to reduce CO_2 emissions by 450

> *Refrigerators with freezers on top use 10 to 25 percent less energy than side-by-side models.*

Recycled Refrigerators

You might balk at the suggestion of moving up to a more efficient refrigerator because you don't like the thought of adding the old one to the town dump. In fact, with the spread of recycling programs around the country, only about 5 percent of a discarded refrigerator will end up in a landfill.

> *Current Energy Star–qualified models are about 40 percent more efficient than conventional models built before 2001, and 50 percent more efficient than those from before 1993.*

pounds a year. When shopping for a refrigerator, check the yellow EnergyGuide label for estimates of how much electricity a particular model will use.

Keep It Simple and Save

If you are in the market for a new refrigerator, consider whether you are paying an energy premium for certain styles and features.

- Refrigerators with freezers on top use 10 to 25 percent less energy than side-by-side models.

- Consider skipping the icemaker and dispenser; they increase energy use by 14 to 20 percent. Plus they can raise the sticker price by $75 to $250, and CR surveys show that they increase the likelihood that your refrigerator will need repair.

- Manual-defrost freezers use half as much energy as those with automatic defrost, but the trick is that you should remember to defrost before the ice gets to be $\frac{1}{4}$ inch thick. As the ice builds up, the efficiency of the freezer goes down.

Recommended Refrigerators

For a rundown of the top-performing refrigerators in CR's tests, go to *www.Consumer Reports.org/energy* and click on Refrigerator Ratings. The highest-rated refrigerators did a particularly good job of maintaining consistently cold temperatures.

Refrigerator Maintenance

Refrigerators may seem maintenance-free, and they very nearly are. You should pay attention to two things, however: the coils and the gaskets. As for the coils, refrigerators use a refrigerant and a compressor to pull heat from inside the fridge, and then release the heat into the air. The release takes place in coils behind the front panel at the bottom of the refrigerator. Most people avoid pulling off the panel

because it gets pretty dirty back there. But the dirt and dust act as an insulator, keeping some of the heat from escaping. At least once a year, brush the dust away with a brush made for the job and sold at appliance and hardware stores.

Newer refrigerators have gaskets that should last the life of the unit. But if you have an older model, another problem may develop: The gaskets around the edges of the doors can begin to crack and no longer seal properly. Warm, moist air gets into your freezer or fridge, causing ice to build up and increasing the amount of electricity the unit uses.

■ ■ ■ Look for a Retainer Strip Before You Leap

If your gasket is held in place by a retaining strip, empty the refrigerator door before you change the gasket—the weight of the food is enough to warp the door. And since the retaining strip provides rigidity, loosening the entire strip at once can also cause the door to warp. Loosen the screws a few at a time, pull out the gasket, and retighten the screws before moving on to the next few screws.

The seals are held in place in one of three ways—by hex-head screws that drive into a retaining strip; by a retainer that the gasket fits over; or by a lip on the gasket that snaps into a groove on the door. Whether the gasket screws into the retainer, or fits over it, you loosen or remove the screws to remove the gasket. In the case of a lipped gasket, you just pull the gasket off the door.

Dirty coils can rob your refrigerator of efficiency. To get to the coils, remove the grille at the bottom of the refrigerator. Brush the coils clean using a tapered brush made specially for this purpose, available at appliance stores.

Check the gasket. Open the door and examine the gasket. Cracks or warping will let cold air leak out; that means that the gasket should be replaced. Mildew, like that shown here, is also a sign that cool air is leaking out. Clean the door, and the surface it meets, in mild detergent (not bleach) and water to remove dirt that might be causing a leak. If mildew recurs, replace the gasket.

Remove the gasket if needed. If the gasket is held in place by screws, loosen or remove a few screws at a time and pull off the old gasket. Retighten the screws before loosening the next few. If the gasket is held in place by a lip, like this one, you just pull the whole thing off.

Warm the replacement gasket. Gaskets are usually kinked as a result of having been folded up in their packaging. Make the gasket easier to work with by soaking it in hot water in your sink until the kinks come out.

Put the new gasket in place. On newer doors, a lip on the gasket tucks into the groove on the door. On other doors you will either tuck part of the gasket behind a retainer or put the screws through holes in the gasket.

CLOTHES WASHERS

With washing machines, it is easy to be clean and green. Newer models use less water and less energy than those of the past. And for peak efficiency, wait until you have enough in the hamper to do a full load. For smaller loads in conventional top-loaders, set the water level accordingly. You can also save lots of energy by washing your clothes in cold water. When you wash in hot water, up to 90 percent of the energy used is consumed by your

> *When you wash in hot water, up to 90 percent of the energy used is consumed by your water heater.*

water heater. Although hot water helps to break down tough dirt, cold-water detergents work effectively for normal loads. For some laundry, such as delicates and dark colors that tend to bleed, cold water is actually preferable.

A front-loading washer uses less energy than a top-loader does and therefore costs less to run. But given the higher purchase price of a front-loader, buying one may not make sense economically.

If you're looking for a new washer, front-loading washers save energy because they use less water. But front-loaders cost more than top-loaders, and the energy savings is not likely to be more than $10 a year.

Buying New

On average, Energy Star washers use just half the energy of conventional top-loading models, although energy standards will change in January 2007. And Energy Star models typically require only 18 to 24 gallons of water per load, compared with 40 gallons for conventional top-loaders manufactured before 2007. Judging the energy efficiency of a washer is a bit involved, since getting your clothes ready to wear involves not only this appliance but the water heater and dryer, too. Energy Star calculates a Modified Energy Factor rating, or MEF, which takes into account the energy consumed by all three appliances.

Compared with pre-2007 top-loading machines, front-loaders generally make more frugal use of energy and water. That's because only the bottom of the basin needs to be filled with water in order to wash the clothing. With the majority of top-loading washers, however, the entire basin must be filled.

The Greenest and Cleanest Washers

When shopping for a washer, be guided by the information on Energy Star labels, but also go to *www.ConsumerReports.org/energy* and click on Efficient Washing Machines. These Ratings are somewhat different than those on the Energy Star labels because CONSUMER REPORTS tests the washers with larger loads.

ConsumerReports.org/energy

■ ■ ■ Line-Dry

One of the simplest energy-conserving devices is a length of clothesline. Take advantage of sunny weather by hanging the wash to dry. Your clothes will smell fresh without the perfumes in fabric softeners and anti-static cloths. When the weather is rainy or cold, consider using indoor drying racks. As an added benefit, you'll add some humidity to dry winter air.

If you have two or more loads to do, try to dry them back-to-back while the dryer is still hot. Use a cool-down cycle with the last load to take advantage of the residual heat.

CLOTHES DRYERS

Dryers are simply large heaters that tumble clothing to aerate it. Because most brands use roughly the same amount of energy, the Energy Star program does not rate dryers or suggest particular models. Still, there's a lot you can do to spend less energy on this household chore.

Removing clothing from the dryer when it feels hot or bone dry is a sure sign that energy is being spent for no practical purpose. The laundry ideally should feel just slightly damp, so that it will fully dry as you sort items and put them away. If you have two or more loads to do, try to dry them back-to-back while the dryer is still hot. Use a cool-down cycle only with the last load to take advantage of the residual heat.

Dryer Maintenance

Running your dryer longer than necessary obviously wastes energy, but there are two ways you may be doing just that without even knowing it. First, if there's lint clogging your dryer's lint trap and/or exhaust vent, moisture can't readily escape, so your dryer is forced to run longer to dry your clothes. And second, your dryer may continue running after the clothes have dried. Many newer dryers have a moisture sensor to prevent the second problem, but the sensor won't work correctly unless you keep the exhaust path clear.

Lint buildup in a dryer traps moisture in the machine and wastes energy. The lint tray should be cleaned after every load.

Clean the lint tray. Pull out and clean the lint tray after every load. Even a small buildup of lint makes it more difficult for moisture to escape the dryer.

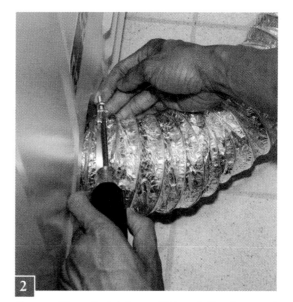

Remove the exhaust hose. Slide out the dryer and remove the hose from the back. The hose is held in place by a metal band on this dryer; sometimes there is a large ring with handles that you pinch to open; sometimes there is a plastic band, which you have to cut through and replace.

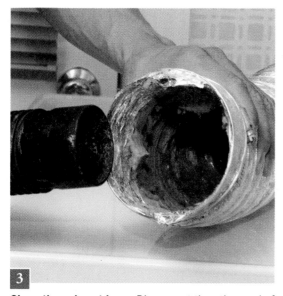

Clean the exhaust hose. Disconnect the other end of the exhaust hose, and vacuum out lint that traps moisture in the dryer. Repeat yearly.

Clean the moisture sensor. If your dryer has a moisture sensor, fabric softener sheets can leave a residue on this device. Clean the sensor occasionally by rubbing it with a soft cloth or a cotton ball dipped in alcohol. The sensor usually consists of two metal strips inside the front edge of the drum—check your owner's manual to find the exact location.

Hot New Dryers

The key feature to look for in a new dryer is a moisture sensor. These are more effective than traditional thermostats in determining when the load is sufficiently dry. That means that the dryer will run for less time with a couple of advantages: You'll use less energy, and your clothes will suffer less wear from tumbling in the dryer. Check product literature or ConsumerReports.org if you aren't sure which technology is used by a particular dryer. About half of the models now on the market are equipped with moisture sensors.

> ### Dryer Recommendations
> CONSUMER REPORTS has found that extra features generally don't improve a dryer's performance. Note that gas-heated dryers cost more initially, but cost less to run. For a look at CONSUMER REPORTS' Ratings of dryers, go to *www.Consumer Reports.org/energy* and click on Dryers.
>
> **ConsumerReports-org/energy**

RANGES

It may seem that electric ranges have taken over the American home kitchen, but gas stoves are making something of a comeback. That's partly due to the fashionable look of professional gas ranges, which CONSUMER REPORTS has found to be not particularly suited for home use and possibly more prone to repairs. Another reason is economic: When equipped with electronic ignition, as all new models are, instead of pilot lights, gas ranges cost less than half as much to use as electric ranges. Pilot flames are tiny, but they're always on, and they increase gas consumption by about 30 percent.

Repair or Replace?

It's usually worth fixing a range if you've had it for seven years or less, and always a sound decision if it's no more than three years old.

A gas stove that has an electronic ignition (instead of a pilot light) costs less than half as much to operate as an electric stove.

■ ■ Convert to Convection?

On average, convection ovens use about 20 percent less energy than conventional models. Unlike "regular" ovens, convection ovens have both a heat source and a fan that circulates the heat throughout the oven. Blowing the hot air on the food makes it cook more quickly.

Range Recommendations

For a look at CONSUMER REPORTS' Ratings of electric, gas, and dual-fuel models (with a gas stovetop and an electric oven), go to *www.ConsumerReports.org/energy* and click on Stoves and Ovens.

ConsumerReports·org/energy

Induction stoves, the latest in electric cooktop technology, cook by delivering electromagnetic energy directly to steel or iron cookware. Cutting a frying pan in half shows how this works—the egg cooks in the pan but remains raw over the burner, which remains cool. Energy usage doesn't vary much among electric range technologies, so don't make energy saving a criterion when choosing among electric ranges.

Microwaves

Microwave ovens have become a common fixture in the kitchen, heating food in seconds and using only about one-third the energy of a conventional oven. They give off little waste heat, which can be a plus on hot summer days.

A sensor helps prevent over- or undercooking by determining when the food is done based on infrared light or the steam emitted by food. The small premium you pay for a sensor is worth it.

■ ■ ■ Microwave Maintenance

Clean the microwave's interior and exterior with a damp rag and kitchen cleaner. If food stains and grime are tough to remove, try microwaving a dish containing a solution of water and white vinegar for a couple of minutes, then wiping down the interior with a dish cloth or sponge.

Microwave Recommendations

When shopping for a microwave, look for models that use sensors to determine the appropriate amount of cooking time. This feature detects either infrared light or moisture emitted by the food and then automatically shuts off the oven. For CONSUMER REPORTS' microwave Ratings go to *www.ConsumerReports .org/energy* and click on Microwave Recommendations.

ConsumerReports.org/energy

Microwave ovens use a fraction of the energy required by a regular oven, and they cook food in a fraction of the time, making them both economical and convenient.

DISHWASHERS

As with washing machines, the biggest expense in dishwashers is heating the water, accounting for about 80 percent of the energy consumed. You'll pay more for a dishwasher with a booster heater, but those models allow you to lower the home's water heater to 120° F, for greater overall efficiency.

Don't wash dishes by hand. An efficient dishwasher can use less water than washing dishes by hand, no matter how frugal you are at the faucet. If you don't like leaving dirty dishes around between washing, run the dishwasher's rinse-and-hold cycle,

which uses only about 2 gallons of water, compared with 4 gallons typical for hand-washing.

Tips for Energy-Saving Dishwashing

Getting your dishwasher to use less energy is a matter of asking it—as well as the person who loads it—to do less.

▪ Use the air-dry function instead of the heat-dry, to save electricity. If your model doesn't have the air-dry feature, you can open the dishwasher door at the end of the cycle to allow the heated dishes to dry on their own.

An efficient dishwasher can use less water than washing by hand. This not only saves water, it saves energy. About 80 percent of the energy used by a dishwasher goes into heating the water.

Dishwasher Maintenance

You'll not only get cleaner dishes by keeping your dishwasher clean, you'll save energy. Washing dishes by hand to remove debris the washer missed uses extra hot water. Trying to remove the debris by running the dishes through a second time uses electricity and hot water, and it usually fails.

The heart of most problems is one of two things: The spray arm isn't shooting water and soap at the dishes because it's clogged, or the dirty water is draining too slowly and ends up being part of the second wash cycle or the rinse cycle.

Choosing the right soap makes a difference, too. CONSUMER REPORTS has found that using a dishwashing soap with enzymes helps get your dishes clean the first time around—and that saves both energy and money.

Some dishwashers come with half-load setting, but this can be an energy waster because two half-loads use more water than one full load. If you want to do smaller loads, consider buying a compact dishwasher.

Dishwasher Recommendations

For more information on choosing an energy-efficient dishwasher, go to *www.Consumer Reports.org/energy* and click on Dishwashers. Note that CONSUMER REPORTS' Ratings are based on tests with even heavier loads than those used by the Energy Star program.

ConsumerReports.org/energy

Check the water temperature. Dishwashers need water that's at least 120° in order to clean well. Run hot water until the temperature stabilizes, checking with a thermometer. If the temperature is less than 120° (such as the 115.8° F shown here), turn up the setting on your home's water heater.

Take out the lower tray. The lower tray, which usually lifts out, and needs to be removed to get to the food filter and spray arm.

Remove the spray arm. Spray arms vary from maker to maker and machine to machine. Most spray arms lift off after you take out a center screw, like this one, which is often covered by a plastic hub. Remove the spray arm as directed by your owner's manual.

Clean the spray arm. Clean the water sprayer once a month. If it becomes clogged with detergent and minerals from the water, remove it and soak it in warm white vinegar.

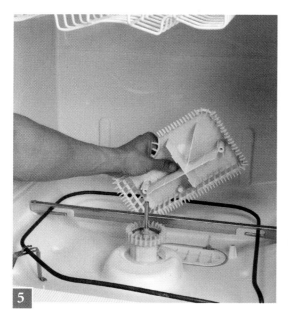

Clean the filter. Some of the more expensive dishwashers have a filter that you have to pull out and clean manually; they're quieter than those with grinders that chop up the debris before washing it down the drain. Remove and clean the filter as recommended in the owner's manual.

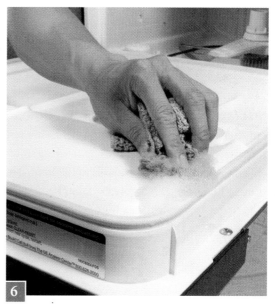

Clean the gasket. To keep water from leaking out of the machine and causing problems, wash the gasket around the door with dish detergent and water. If you see cracks and gaps that might create leaks, call the manufacturer's customer-service number and ask whether you can fix it yourself or should call in a pro to repair it.

WATER HEATERS

That water heater working quietly and unnoticed in your basement is consuming about 20 percent of the energy that your home uses. That's not too surprising when you consider that it is serving every hot-water tap and showerhead in the house, in addition to the dishwasher and washing machine. It could be worse—and it was, in years past. Insulation has improved, in response to national appliance-efficiency standards.

The basic strategy for saving energy dollars on hot water is fourfold: Use cooler water, use less hot water by installing water-saver shower-heads, make sure your water heater and pipes are adequately insulated, and maintain the unit.

Check the Thermostat

The U.S. Department of Energy says that a setting of 120° F is generally hot enough. Dishwashers function best with 140° water, but many newer models have temperature boosters that bring a cooler supply up to that level. So the first thing to do is make sure the water heater's thermostat is set at 120° or 140°, depending on whether you have a dishwasher with a temperature booster.

Insulate Your Water Heater and Pipes

Put your hand on the side of your water heater. If it's warm, you can save money by covering it with an insulating jacket, available at any hardware store or home center. This is especially effective for older water heaters with less built-in insulation, and for heaters located in unheated spaces.

> *That water heater working quietly and unnoticed in your basement is consuming about 20 percent of the energy that your home uses.*

■ ■ ■ Install Low-Flow Fixtures

Showerheads manufactured before 1992 sometimes used more than twice the water used by the low-flow showerheads that are made today. Replacing an older shower-head with a modern low-flow head could obviously save both water and the energy required to heat it. You can't tell by looking whether your current showerhead is low flow, but you can run a quick test. Put a 1-gallon bucket under the showerhead and turn on the shower at the water pressure you normally use. If it takes less than 20 seconds to fill the bucket, install a low-flow showerhead. You'll have a wide choice—federal regulations mandate that all new showerheads are low-flow.

Remove the old showerhead with a wrench. If it is difficult to remove, protect the pipe coming out of the wall with a rag, and hold it firmly with pliers. Turn only the wrench that's on the old showerhead.

Wrap the threads with a few turns of Teflon tape to prevent leaks once the new head is installed.

Thread the new head onto the stem by hand until it stops, then tighten a quarter- to a half-turn with a wrench.

It takes just a few minutes to put an insulation jacket in place—just follow the directions on the package. Be careful not to cover the thermostat or the air intake on gas water heaters.

Now that you have made sure that the water will stay hot while it's waiting in the tank, the next step is to keep it hot while it travels through the pipes. Insulate exposed hot-water pipes with foam pipe insulation. See "Insulating Hot-Water Pipes," page 114.

Repair or Replace?

While a corroded, leaking water heater tank isn't salvageable, a leaky drain valve or pressure-relief valve or a worn-out electric heating element can be fixed. But replacing the heater may make more sense.

Find out by getting a repair estimate. Then weigh that amount against the $175 to $350 plus installation you'll pay for a new heater with installation. Consider repairing a water heater if the labor cost, which warranties often exclude, averages less than $50 per year for each remaining year of the

warranty. Otherwise put the money you'd pay for the plumber's visit toward installing a new unit, especially if yours is out of warranty.

When looking for a new heater, CONSUMER REPORTS suggests that you pay attention to the "first-hour" rating (FHR) on the EnergyGuide tag. It tells how much hot water can be delivered in an hour of use, and it may be that a smaller tank will be as productive as a larger one. CONSUMER REPORTS sawed open 28 gas and electric water heaters to see what was inside. The finding? Models with longer warranties typically were better products, with thicker insulation, larger heating elements or burners, and corrosion-resistant metal rods (called anodes).

Electric heaters tend to cost less, but natural-gas models cost roughly half as much to run. If your house isn't connected to a natural-gas line, propane tanks may offer another way to save. See the chart "Water Heaters Compared," page 94, for more information.

Beyond the Conventional

When buying a new water heater, the choices extend beyond the conventional tank you probably grew up with.

- **On-demand water heaters** (also called instantaneous or tankless heaters) warm the water when you turn on the tap. Since they only heat water when you turn on the tap, they save the energy required to keep hot water on standby in a tank. There are three types of on-demand heaters: central, individual, and boiler-based.

  A central on-demand water heater is a single tankless heater capable of heating water for the whole house. While these can be significantly more efficient than a conventional water heater, they may not be able to keep up with high demand.

(Continued on page 94)

Removing Sediment from Your Water Heater

The thousands of gallons of water that come into your house every year bring a bit of sediment with them—it may be sand, or it may be dissolved lime that settles out of the water. In any event, the sediment can insulate the water from the heat source, and it should be periodically removed to improve energy efficiency and to prolong the life of the water heater.

1 **Turn off the water heater.** Running the heater while flushing it wastes energy by heating water that's going down the drain, and can also burn out the heating element. If you have an electric water heater or a gas unit with electronic ignition, turn it off at the breaker panel, fuse box, or cutoff box, if there is one. If you have a gas unit with a gas pilot, turn it to "pilot".

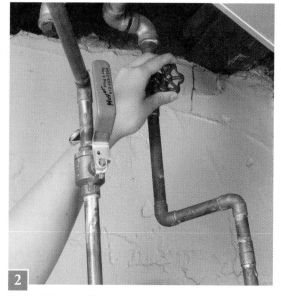

Shut off the cold water. Turn the cutoff valve in the line that supplies cold water to the water heater. Initially, you want the tank to drain without refilling.

Open a hot-water tap. Open a tap anywhere in the house. This will allow air to displace the water in the tank, letting it drain more quickly and thoroughly.

Open the draincock. Put a hose on the draincock at the bottom of the tank, and run it to a drain. Open the spigot and let the tank drain. Be careful: The water will initially be a minimum of 120° F and could scald you.

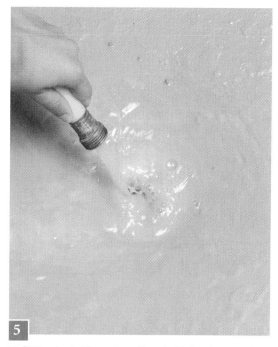

Refill the tank. The water will probably be cloudy at first, and will stop running once the tank drains. When the tank stops draining, open the valve on the cold-water supply line and let the water rinse the tank. When the water runs clear, close the spigot and the hot-water tap. Then turn the gas or electricity back on.

Individual on-demand heaters heat water for a single faucet, and are connected to the plumbing near that faucet. Most typically, these units are electric and they can be a good choice for a large house with baths far from the water source, especially if you are heating water with electricity anyway. But since electricity costs more than gas, they may not save you money if your main water heater uses gas.

Furnace-boiler-based on-demand heaters route the pipes through a heat exchanger in the boiler where the water is heated as needed. Because

the furnace needs to operate in order to heat the water, their average efficiency can be low, especially in warmer climates.

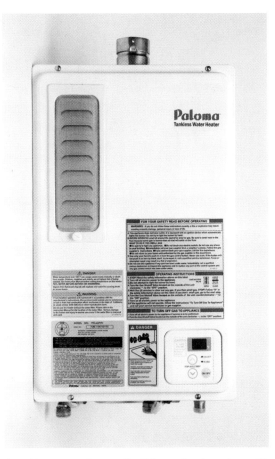

A tankless water heater like this one heats water as it's needed rather than keeping a large supply of hot water on hand. A unit attached to a single faucet can save up to half the energy that a conventional tank requires.

Back to the Future with Solar

A century ago, solar water heaters were a common sight on roofs in parts of Florida and Southern California. They are regaining popularity, thanks in part to improved reliability. Typically they are used with conventional heaters as a backup to meet periods of peak demand and when there is a stretch of cloudy weather.

On average, a solar water heater can annually spare the environment 2.5 tons of carbon dioxide, a problematic greenhouse gas. As for dollar savings, a solar heater can reduce annual water heating bills by up to a few hundred dollars and typically will pay for itself in four to seven years, depending on the climate.

Water Heaters Compared		
Water Heating System	Cost, with installation	Yearly energy cost	Total cost over 13 years
Conventional gas storage	$380	$179	$2,707
Conventional electric storage	350	410	5,680
On-demand electric (2 units)	600	414	5,982
Indirect, with efficient boiler	600	100	1,900
Electric heat pump	1,200	140	3,020
Solar with electric backup	2,500	125	4,125

■ **Indirect water heaters** are another way of using the home heating system to provide warm water. The boiler circulates hot water through a coil in an adjacent storage tank. Because there is a supply of hot water on hand, the boiler doesn't have to cycle frequently, improving energy efficiency. In fact, this can be the least-expensive way to heat water, assuming the boiler is new and highly efficient. You can add on a storage tank for indirect heating, but a more common course is to buy the tank when replacing an older boiler with a new model.

■ **Heat-pump water heaters** save half or more of the energy used by conventional electrical units. As with home-heating heat pumps, they draw their heat from the air. These heaters can be purchased with built-in tanks or as an add-on to an existing water tank.

LIGHTING

Although a lightbulb may not look like an energy-devouring appliance, collectively the home's lighting represents a good chunk of your electric bill. You can save substantially by making changes in the types of bulbs you use and their placement around the home. There are three general ways

to light your home. Balancing them, or replacing one with another, could save you energy dollars.

■ **Ambient lighting** is the overall illumination that spreads throughout a space. A well-lit room can seem cheerful, and you can walk around in it safely, but you need a lot of watts to do the job.

■ **Task lighting** is focused on a particular area, such as over a kitchen counter, on each side of a bathroom mirror, or over a chair you use for reading. By having task lighting that you can turn on in frequently used areas, you save energy because there's less need to rely on ambient fixtures. Task lighting also may make a setting seem more intimate and cozy; compare the difference between cafeteria lighting and the subtle pockets of illumination in a high-end restaurant.

■ **Accent lighting** is used aesthetically to bring attention to artwork or play up architectural features of the home.

If task and accent lighting also provide some of your ambient lighting needs, you can create a more dramatic atmosphere without increasing energy costs, and it may even be possible to use less energy.

Bright Choices: Compact Fluorescent Lamps

It might seem that simply switching to energy-efficient lightbulbs couldn't make that much difference. But compact fluorescents (CFLs) really are a new twist on the old incandescent bulb. CFLs take the cool-burning, energy-conserving advantages of long fluorescent tubes and reconfigure them in a small (if odd-looking) screw-in bulb.

CFLs are far more efficient than incandescent bulbs, which put off about 90 percent of the energy they consume as waste heat. This means that a

Screw In a Bulb, Save the Planet

Unlike adopting other energy-conserving measures, changing a lightbulb is as simple as ... well, changing a lightbulb. If every household in the U.S. replaced the five most frequently used incandescents with compact fluorescent lamps, the lower electricity consumption would reduce power-plant emissions equal to the greenhouse gasses generated by 8 million cars. Because you're replacing high-use bulbs, the financial payback is big—about $60 a year.

15-watt CFL will do the job of a 60-watt incandescent bulb, and a 25-watt CFL will provide as much light as a 100-watt incandescent. A CFL bulb will last many times as long as an incandescent, and their cost has dropped dramatically—

Compact fluorescent bulbs are fluorescent bulbs that screw into standard sockets. They provide the same amount of light as incandescent lights but use a fraction of the energy.

Solar Savings

The cheapest—and easiest—source of electricity for outdoor lighting is the sun. Locations that receive at least several hours of direct sunlight a day are candidates for solar fixtures that you simply stick in the ground. That isn't to say the yard will be lit up brilliantly, or that the lights will remain on all night, but these fixtures can be ideal for defining a pathway. Check the packaging of solar lighting fixtures for the "nightly run time," and note how many hours of direct sunlight the unit requires for optimum performance. In the warmer months, vegetation can block the sun; and in winter, the sun is both lower in the sky and weaker, potentially cutting the run time by 30 to 50 percent.

you can buy them in bulk for as little as $1 to $2 each. Look for Energy Star-rated CFLs—they list how long they will last.

Turn Out the Lights

An easy way to save on lighting is to flick the switch when you leave a room. You should do that routinely for conventional incandescent bulbs. For fluorescents, however, which operate more efficiently once they're warmed up, only turn them off if you expect to be out of the room more than 15 minutes. For incandescents, both wall switches and light fixtures themselves can be fitted with motion or infrared sensors. When no one's around, the lights go off automatically. Note that CFLs may not work with these sensors.

There's a middle ground between turning lights on and off: You can use dimmers to lower light levels when you don't need (or want) brilliantly lit surroundings. For incandescent bulbs, all you need to do is replace a standard wall switch with a dimmer. You'll use less electricity and bulbs will last longer, though the efficiency of the bulb is reduced somewhat. Better yet, simply turn off some light fixtures if not needed or use a

Low-voltage systems are an inexpensive, efficient way to shed a bit of light where it is needed most, particularly along walkways and steps. A motion-sensor floodlight bathes the area in light, but only when there is movement in the area.

strategically placed table or floor lamp to provide low-level lighting.

For conventional fluorescent fixtures, on the other hand, you need a special dimming ballast for each fixture, but efficiency remains the same at lower light levels. You can't dim most CFLs that screw into fixtures designed for incandescent bulbs. There are a few models sold at retail that can be dimmed, but they are more expensive than other CFLs.

Daylighting Costs Nothing

To spend less on electric lighting, look for ways to take advantage of daylight. Light-colored, translucent curtains can transform harsh sunlight into a soft glow that illuminates every corner of the room. Simply rolling a lighter color of paint on the walls will brighten up the home. If you plan to remodel and there are parts of your house that are chronically dark, consider installing a light tube. From the outside, this device looks like a conventional skylight, but the light travels down a flexible tube that can be positioned to illuminate a dark hallway or a bathroom without a window. On a sunny day, a light tube can provide light equivalent to about 100 watts. Taking advantage of daylight does more than save electricity: There is research to suggest that people feel better and function more efficiently in rooms with plenty of natural light.

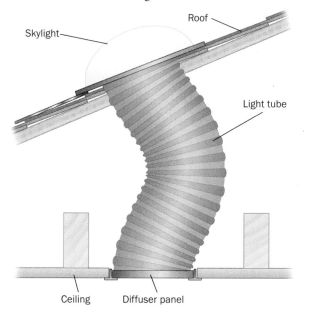

A skylight with a flexible tube that has a highly polished interior can add light to a room without the elaborate framing that's required by a traditional skylight.

Light Up the Outside

Conventional floodlights are widely used decoratively and for security, but they draw a lot of current with their powerful incandescent bulbs. You can save energy by using fixtures with light sensors that turn the lights on at night, or fixtures with motion sensors that turn on the lights when someone is in the vicinity at night. Switch to CFLs. They use fewer kilowatts, and with their longer life, they make trips up a ladder for replacement a less-frequent chore. If you've got decorative natural gas lamps, turn them off. They may create atmosphere, but they don't put off much light—and they are remarkably wasteful. Keeping just eight of them burning year-round consumes enough natural gas to heat an average-sized home for an entire winter.

If you want to light a path rather than a large area, use a low-voltage system. Because there's relatively little juice flowing through the wires, it's not necessary to hire an electrician for the installation. You simply plug in a transformer (ideally one with a timer), run wires between several fixtures along the path, and then bury the wires in a shallow trench. Home centers sell kits with a transformer and several lights, as well as the individual components, so that you can assemble your own system.

Lantern. Spreads light over general area. Well-suited for lighting a garden or providing decoration. Not the best choice for lighting a walkway because light isn't always focused on the ground.

Spotlight. Directs light to a focused area. Well-suited for visual accent, focusing a wash of light onto a tree or entryway.

Path spotlight. Fixtures aim light downward in one direction. Well-suited for pathways.

Tier. Vanes direct light downward in a fairly small area. Well-suited for lighting a garden. Suitable for narrow pathways if lights are placed no more than 3 to 4 feet apart.

Spread. Directs light downward in a circle, illuminating everything in a wide radius. Well-suited for lighting a path and bordering plants. Not a good choice in an expanse of empty lawn or close to the house foundation.

Bollard. Post-shaped fixture directs light to the sides. Well-suited for low-level light in gardens and flower beds.

Clusters of low-voltage landscape lighting can give you a lot more for your kilowatt dollar, but you'll want to space them to their best advantage. Landcape lighting is most effective when used sparingly to create an interesting pattern of light and shadow. One spotlight to call attention to a tree or wash a wall is effective; several can be overkill. On the other hand, for functional lighting—especially on a garden path or sidewalk—you want to strive for uniform illumination.

IMPROVING HOME HEATING AND COOLING

When you're cold, you turn up the thermostat. When you feel hot and wilted, you turn it down. So, if your home always feels either chilly or steamy, it's only natural to blame the furnace or air conditioning system.

Not so fast. The problem may be elsewhere. And that's great news because all those other problems are usually a lot cheaper to fix than replacing your furnace or central-air-conditioning unit. That's why we spent the earlier chapters of this book telling you how to save money with insulation, weatherstripping, windows, and doors. Each helps reduce the load on your heating and cooling systems and may make upgrades or replacements to the system unnecessary.

Of course furnaces and AC systems do wear out. If that happens to you, take consolation in the fact that you'll most likely be replacing an inefficient furnace with a remarkably efficient one that can result in big savings over time. Back in 1972, for example, furnaces were 63 percent efficient on average. That jumped to 83 percent by 1995, and now there are models that are more than 95 percent efficient. Heating and cooling account for 56 percent of the energy consumed by a typical household. You'll find advice on new furnaces later in the chapter.

■ ■ ■ Seal Up, Then Scale Down

Before buying a new furnace or AC system based on your home's current needs, take the opportunity to seal your home and add insulation. You may be able to choose a smaller unit, meaning a lower purchase price now and reduced utility bills for years to come. Look for leaky seams in the ducts, and seal them with mastic and fiberglass mesh; then insulate the ducts that pass through unconditioned spaces. This step alone can cut heating and cooling costs by 40 percent. See "Sealing Ductwork," page 36, for more information on sealing this distribution system.

> *"On most systems, you can cut heating or cooling costs as much as 20 percent by lowering your home's thermostat 5° F at night and 10° F during the day."*

SAVING WITH YOUR EXISTING HOME HEATING SYSTEM

There is a lot you can do now to get more heat out of your heating system and lower your utility bills. Brainy thermostats, billing options, and sound maintenance all can help keep your home comfortable and healthful at minimum cost.

Quality Programming

All home heating and cooling systems, from sophisticated heat exchangers to attaché-case-sized space heaters, are governed by thermostats. How this "brain" works is crucial to the efficiency of your system. On most systems, you can cut heating or cooling costs as much as 20 percent by lowering your home's thermostat 5° F at night and 10° F during the day when nobody is home, or raising it during the air-conditioning season. (Heat pumps are the exception to the rule: Turning them on and off during their complicated heating cycle can actually raise your heating and cooling bills.) You can accomplish this savings with a simple thermostat if you can remember to change the setting several times a day. But few of us are that diligent, and the result is a heating bill that's higher than necessary.

Enter the programmable (or "setback") thermostat, a good, inexpensive way to automate the process. Like any thermostat, this is basically a thermometer that turns a system on and off as temperatures fluctuate. The difference is that programmable models let you set different temperatures for various times of day. Many models let you program each day of the week separately

The Benefits of a Thinking Thermostat

To learn how much you potentially can save with a programmable thermostat, go to *www.ConsumerReports.org/energy* and click on Savings Calculator–Programmable Thermostats.

ConsumerReports.org/energy

Mercury Alert

Older thermostats are likely to contain mercury, a silvery liquid that is contained in a glass tube as part of the switching mechanism. Mercury is a known neurotoxin, and efforts are under way at the state and federal levels to prevent it from being spread to the environment from discarded thermostats. Although a typical device contains just 3 or 4 grams of the metal, the EPA estimates that some 230 tons of it have been used in the manufacture of thermostats. In Illinois alone, it's thought that between 8,000 and 132,000 thermostats are tossed out each year.

For information on recycling options, go to *www.ConsumerReports. org/energy* and click on Mercury in Thermostats.

ConsumerReports.org/energy

for four temperature changes per day. This means, for example, that during the heating season you can have the temperature go up when you awake in the morning, down when your family leaves for work and/or school, up again before you arrive home, and down after you go to bed. Weekends, or any day of the week you don't go to work, can be scheduled differently. During the cooling season you can set the temperature higher during periods when you are asleep or away.

Some programmable thermostats can even tell you when it's time to change your furnace or AC filter, and some include a humidistat, which can be useful for northern homes in the winter. If your home has several heating or cooling zones,

you'll need a setback thermostat for each to maximize energy savings.

Public utility companies advise their customers that Energy Star-labeled programmable thermostats can maximize a homeowner's savings and cut home heating and cooling bills by between 20 and 30 percent over the course of a year.

Older thermostats were simply thermometers that turned the heating or cooling system on and off as the temperature changed. Unlike the sophisticated models that are available today, the old thermostats left it to you to remember to turn the dial cooler or warmer when the time came.

Installing a Programmable Thermostat

Replacing a standard thermostat with a money-saving programmable thermostat is a simple job. All you need is a screwdriver, a drill, and 5 or 10 minutes.

Though the specifics vary from thermostat to thermostat, the cover pops off the old thermostat one way or another, exposing a couple of screws that you back out to remove the body of the thermostat from the wall. A few more screws hold wires that run to the furnace. If the thermostat controls the heat supply and nothing else, there will be only two wires; if it also controls a central air conditioner, there'll be more. Knowing which goes where on the new thermostat is straightforward—the wires are color-coded, and the screws in programmable thermostats are labeled.

You will probably need to drill new mounting holes for the thermostat. Screws are usually included with the thermostat, along with plastic anchors that will help hold them in the drywall.

Note that the thin low-voltage wires connecting most thermostats are relatively safe to work with. But full household current may run through a thermostat that governs electric baseboard heaters, and only an electrician or an HVAC contractor should handle replacement of those.

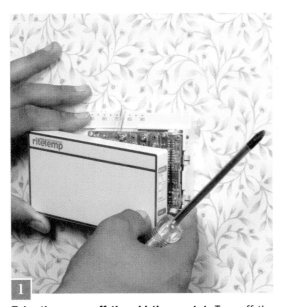

Take the cover off the old thermostat. Turn off the power supply to the existing thermostat at the home's circuit breaker, at the fuse box, or at the furnace cutoff switch, if there is one. If the thermostat is on an electric baseboard heater, hire an electrician or an HVAC contractor instead of doing the job yourself.

Remove the wires. Unscrew the wires from their terminals. If the wires aren't color-coded, label them with tape, marking each piece with the letter of the nearby screw terminal.

Unscrew the mounting screws. Remove the screws holding the body of the thermostat to the wall, and take it off the wall. The wires will sometimes try to slide back through the hole in the wall that they pass through; if so, tape them temporarily in place.

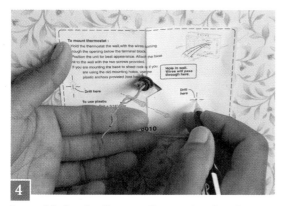

4 Lay out holes for the new thermostat. Put the template that comes with the new thermostat on the wall. Poke a pencil through the marks on the template to show where on the wall the screws should go.

5 Drill holes for anchors. The package will include small plastic anchors that you put in the holes to help hold the screws in place. You won't need them if you happen to drill into a stud. Drill holes in the wall for the anchors—the package directions will tell you what size holes to drill.

6 Put the anchors in the wall. Push the anchors into the holes. Plaster and drywall are fragile, and without the anchors or a stud behind, the thermostat would come loose with normal use.

7 Screw the thermostat to the wall. Feed the wires through the opening for them in the body of the thermostat. Screw the body to the wall, driving the screws into the plastic anchors, or the studs.

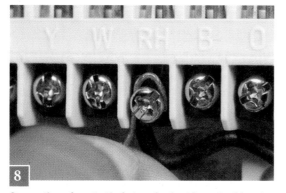

8 Screw the wires to their terminals. After attaching the wires, install a battery if needed.

9 Mount the new thermostat. Attach the cover to the body of the thermostat, turn the power back on, and program the device as directed in the manufacturer's instructions.

Billing Savvy

If you heat with oil, you have several buying options. The one that's best depends on your needs and on the direction that wholesale oil prices take during the heating season—something that you can't predict. Here are the choices and what you need to know.

Full-service. Signing up with a full-service dealer offers convenient features such as automatic delivery, a maintenance contract with 24-hour emergency service, and a budget plan that spreads payments out equally. You also can choose a fixed price, which remains the same no matter what happens to wholesale prices, or a capped price, which can actually fall if wholesale prices decline below a certain level. Because full-service customers are contractually bound to a single company for the heating season, they can't comparison-shop, often making a full-service contract the most expensive option. If your capped price doesn't seem to go down as oil prices decline generally, ask questions. Insiders tell CONSUMER REPORTS that some dealers rarely pass lower prices on to consumers unless the customers complain.

Cash on delivery (C.O.D.). With this option, you comparison-shop among several companies whenever you need a delivery. While inconvenient, this offers the best chance for savings. (The draw-back is that if wholesale oil prices rise unexpectedly, you could end up paying more than if you had locked in a price with a full-service dealer. You also must carefully monitor your tank because you'll pay a premium if you run out of oil or need immediate delivery. Some C.O.D companies have Web sites that advertise the current daily price. Find out whether any of the C.O.D. companies in your area offer 24-hour emergency service; if not, line up a heating contractor who does.

Buying groups. With fees of around $15 to $30, buying groups offer the convenience of automatic delivery and, in many cases, a maintenance contract with 24-hour emergency service. While some may have fixed or capped prices, most customers are on a daily price that's calculated using a formula that the dealers agree to ahead of time. That usually translates to a savings of around 20 to 30 cents a gallon off a full-service company's regular daily price. Nonprofit buying groups may offer better savings than the for-profit variety. If there's no buying group in your area, try setting one up through your church, civic group, or homeowners' association.

No matter how you buy. Ask your oil company about discounts, typically available to senior citizens, those who pay quickly after a delivery, and those with large oil tanks (500-gallon or larger). One caution: Some companies offer discounts to those who pay weeks or even months in advance. But prepaying can prove disastrous if the company unexpectedly goes out business, as some have done.

HOME-HEATING-SYSTEM MAINTENANCE AND TUNE-UP

Before finding ways to spend less on heating your home, you need to understand where that heat comes from. What does the system run on, and how does it distribute warmth through the house? Here's a quick look at the various systems.

A *forced-air furnace* sounds simple enough—and it is, at least in principle. Oil, gas, or (less commonly) electricity is used to heat air, which is

■ ■ Finding Heating Oil for Less

Some heating-oil dealers post their daily prices on the Internet. Also, your local government's Web site might list the various oil prices in your area for easy cost comparisons.

distributed through the home via ducts. If you have a forced-air system, you'll know it by the ducts—some to deliver the air and others to return the cooled air to the furnace. If the system is coupled with air conditioning, the same ductwork circulates cooling air.

A *hot-water* or *steam-boiler* system works by distributing hot water or, at a higher temperature, steam. To transfer heat to the living spaces, hot water passes through radiators, baseboard heaters, or pipes embedded in a room's surfaces, most commonly the floor. Radiators are used for steam, as well. The hot water or steam travels in a loop that returns to the boiler be heated again.

An *electric-baseboard* system operates something like a toaster. Electric current runs through wires that resist its travel, creating heat. These wires may be in baseboard units or larger wall-mounted panels.

A *heat pump* uses electricity to transfer heat between the inside of the home and the outdoors. The flow potentially can go either way. In cold weather, the heat pump draws heat from the outside air, a body of water, or the ground and distributes it indoors. In hot weather, the system moves heat from the living space to the outdoors. In most homes, both warm and cool air are distributed by ducts.

Basic Maintenance

Home-heating systems tend be out of sight and out of mind. And that's as it should be, since maintenance tasks for modern units are few and infrequent. But to get the most from your heating dollar, and to keep the household safe, you'll need either to keep an eye on how the system is operating or regularly bring in a reliable technician to do the job. It's best to arrange for an appointment for a checkup when you're least likely to think of it—before the weather turns chilly and those technicians get too busy. Make a note on your calendar to schedule a visit.

■ ■ ■ If the CO Detector Sounds Its Alarm...

The EPA cautions that a CO detector alone doesn't keep your household safe. Only a thorough inspection of the heating system can ensure that carbon monoxide gas will not endanger you. Here's what to do if the alarm goes off:

■ Confirm that the alarm is for the CO detector and not for a smoke detector.

■ If people in the household suddenly get a headache or feel flulike symptoms, take them out of the house and call for medical assistance.

■ Open windows and doors to bring in fresh air. Turn off any system or appliance that might be the source of CO, including the furnace and gas water heater, range, oven, dryer, or space heater.

■ Call for a technician to check these systems and appliances, as well as chimneys, to see that they are operating properly.

Most important, watch out for potentially unsafe conditions. Inspect pipes and chimneys for leaky joints, holes, and blockages that might allow CO gas to escape into the home, and install a carbon-monoxide alarm. Also examine gas and oil piping for leaks.

CO Alarms

Carbon-monoxide gas kills about 500 people in the United States each year, and CO alarms are now required in some states. These devices have improved in recent years, as CONSUMER REPORTS has found. For an evaluation of models, go to *www.ConsumerReports.org/energy* and click on Carbon Monoxide Alarms.

Forced-Air System

If your home is heated by forced air, whether from a furnace or a heat pump, the distribution system involves particular maintenance tasks.

■ Have a technician inspect the furnace heat exchanger and chimney for cracks that might allow CO into the home.

■ Check the furnace air filters during each month of operation, and clean or replace them as needed.

■ A fuel-oil system will usually need to have the heat exchanger cleaned and the oil filter changed.

■ Inspect the ductwork for leaks at seams, transitions, and other joints. Seal small leaks with

Air in the radiator lines keeps hot water from heating the radiators. A radiator key, sold at hardware stores, opens a valve that lets the air escape. When the water runs out of the valve, close it and enjoy the heat.

foil tape, not with ordinary fabric duct tape. For gaps wider than ¼ inch, apply duct mastic as described in "Sealing Ductwork," page 36.

■ Vacuum registers and remove them for cleaning if necessary.

■ Have the ducts cleaned if a visual inspection turns up a substantial amount of dust and debris, or if family members are experiencing unusual allergic reactions or other symptoms.

■ Whether the system is fueled by gas or oil, have the technician clean it thoroughly and give it a tune-up.

Hot-Water System

Just as a forced-hot-air system relies on ducts to deliver its heat, a hot-water boiler needs a network of pipes in good working order.

■ When air gets into the lines and radiator, the system operates inefficiently. Normally, air is automatically separated from the water. In some systems it is stored in an expansion tank that needs to be emptied. In other systems the air is automatically vented. If radiators are not heating up, you can improve the situation by bleeding them, but this probably means the vents or expansion tank needs servicing by a technician. Have the technician check both cold- and hot-system pressure to ensure that the fill valve, the automatic air vents, and the expansion tank are working as they should.

■ Vacuum dust from baseboard fins to allow them to conduct heat readily.

■ Water expands in volume as its temperature rises. To prevent a buildup of pressure from damaging the system, have a technician make

A setback thermostat can be set to automatically turn the heat down at nights or when you're at work, and to turn the heat back up when needed. There's no heat wasted, as a result, and a setback thermometer could cut your heating costs by 20 or 30 percent.

sure that both the pressure-relief valve and the high-limit control are functioning properly.

■ The technician should examine the boiler water pumps for leaks and lubricate the pump and motor if necessary.

Steam System

Like steam-powered locomotives, home steam boilers are largely a thing of the past, although they are still found in older homes. All of the following are jobs for a technician. Note that radiator maintenance is different for one-pipe systems (a single pipe supplies steam and also returns condensed water) than for two-pipe systems (a second pipe returns the condensate).

■ Check steam vents and traps to make sure that steam can freely reach the radiators. In a two-pipe system, traps tend to stick open or closed,

so that some radiators get too hot while others remain cool. The surest remedy is to replace all the traps in the system.

■ A one-pipe system has an automatic air vent on each radiator that bleeds air until steam reaches the vent. If a vent becomes clogged, the radiator won't heat up. To clean an air vent, turn off the steam supply to the radiator, remove the vent, and soak it in a solution of water and vinegar. Replace the vent if this doesn't work.

■ Clean the water in the boiler by skimming the surface and also by draining sediment to improve heat transfer.

■ Test the low-water cutoff safety valve and the high-limit safety control.

■ If you have any float chamber controls, such as a low-water cutoff, drain and clean the chamber.

■ Clean the heat exchanger.

On steam-heat systems, air vents like this one automatically let out trapped air that interferes with the heat. If the vent gets clogged, turn off the heat, remove the vent when the radiator is cold, and soak the vent in water and vinegar before replacing.

Although it's easy to forget about the inner workings of the furnace until something goes wrong, make a point of scheduling annual service visits. Keeping your furnace in good shape will help save you money.

Oil Furnace or Boiler

If you heat with an oil boiler, consider installing an outdoor temperature reset control. These devices adjust the temperature of the water in your boiler based on the outside temperature— when it is warmer outside, the water will be cooler. As a result, the boiler needs to turn on and off less often than it would without the control, minimizing temperature fluctuations and increasing your comfort. It may also increase the efficiency of high-efficiency boilers.

As for annual maintenance, it's crucial to keep the unit burning cleanly and efficiently.

The technician should attend to the following:

- Brush and vacuum the interior.
- Replace the nozzle.
- Clean the pump strainer.
- Replace the oil filter and its gasket.
- Check the pump pressure.
- Test the ignition transformer.
- Lubricate the burner motor, as well as the circulator motor or blower motor.

Heat Pumps

Heat pumps are prone to their own set of problems. In an Energy Star study, more than half of all heat

▓ ▓ ▓ Why a Duct-Cleaning Service?

You may have encountered duct-cleaning services that promise to clear your forced air heating and/or cooling system of bacteria and various contaminants. Unless a physician recommends the procedure to relieve allergy symptoms, you probably should save your money.

pumps were operating inefficiently due to insufficient airflow, leaky ducts, or an improper level of refrigerant.

▓ Seal any small leaks along duct seams with UL-listed foil tape, not with ordinary fabric duct tape. For gaps in other joints, apply duct mastic, as described in "Sealing Ductwork," page 36.

▓ Have the technician clean the evaporator coil to ensure proper airflow.

▓ The tech should check the refrigerant level to make sure that it conforms to the manufacturer's specifications.

▓ Have the technician check the secondary heating elements, reversing valve, and defrost cycle, as well as timers or sensors, depending on the type of system you have.

If the fins on your central air conditioner, window air conditioner, or heat pump get bent, the exchange of heat is less efficient. Straighten them with a fin comb (inset), available at heating, venting, and air-conditioning supply shops. Combs usually have several sets of teeth. Choose the set that matches the spacing of the fins that you are fixing.

Changing a Disposable Furnace Filter

Choosing a furnace air filter is a balancing act between filter efficiency and air resistance. The greater the efficiency, the cleaner the air, but the more likely the filter is to restrict airflow, lessening furnace efficiency and possibly damaging the furnace. Efficiency is measured by something called the Minimum Efficiency Reporting Value (MERV), which is rated on a scale of 1 to 16. The higher the number, the greater the efficiency. Look for the MERV value on the filter when you buy it. The National Air Filtration Association (NAFA) recommends filters with a MERV of 11 or lower for most home furnaces. There are four main types of filters suitable for home use, ranging from MERV 4 to 12:

Disposable fiberglass panels (MERV 4 to 5). These are inexpensive disposable filters, designed primarily to protect the furnace. They will remove only the largest dirt particles from the air, and according to NAFA, tests have shown they're not very good at that. Because they prove little resistance to airflow, however, NAFA says they are the most commonly used filters.

Washable filters (MERV 4 to 5). These are removable and reusable but are generally no more effective at removing dust than disposable fiberglass filters.

Disposable pleated filters (MERV 8). These filters fold the filtering medium into accordion-like pleats. Because of the resulting greater surface area, they can remove up to 50 percent of airborne dust.

Disposable high-efficiency pleated filters (MERV 11 to 12). These remove dust from the air using an electrostatic charge and can be up to 30 times more efficient than panel filters, according to the American Lung Association.

HEPA filters. HEPA (high-efficiency particulate air) filters can remove up to 99 percent of the dust that passes through your furnace. But while more filter means less dust, it also means greater resistance, less airflow, and possible damage to the furnace. Talk with an HVAC professional about the feasibility of using one of these filters.

The dirt in a furnace filter can restrict airflow and have an impact on the performance of your furnace. Clean or replace it every three months during the heating season.

Remove the filter. Turn off the furnace at the fusebox, the circuit breaker, or the furnace cutoff switch. Remove the filter from its housing, which may be inside the furnace, or inside the air return vent, as is the case here.

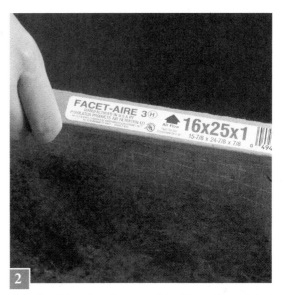

Note the filter size. The size of the filter will be printed somewhere on the cardboard frame. Write down the size of the filter, and get a new one at a hardware store, home center, or HVAC supplier.

Change the Filter Regularly

If you have a forced-air furnace or air conditioning, check the filter regularly to keep dust and dirt from finding their way into the furnace's blower and coil assemblies, and plan to change the filter every three months during heating season. Maintaining the filter is an easy and important way to keep your system running efficiently, saving energy dollars.

According to the Michigan Department of Labor and Economic Growth, most service calls could have been prevented if care had been taken to keep dust and dirt from gumming up the works. If neglected long enough, the motor can be damaged. Check the manufacturer's recommendations for how often to replace disposable filters or clean reusable filters. Note that there may be filters at the system's return ducts, as well as in the furnace's central fan unit, and these should be inspected and cleaned or replaced monthly.

Put the new filter in the furnace. Look for the markings that tell you which side of the filter should face the furnace. Slide the filter back into place, and replace any cover that goes over it.

Cleaning a Reusable Furnace Filter

Reusable filters won't give you air that's any cleaner than a standard fiberglass panel filter will, but they'll save you a trip to the store for a replacement. Because they have a plastic core and a plastic frame, reusable filters can be vacuumed clean, rinsed down with a hose, and then put back in the furnace. Let the filter dry before you put it back in place.

Clean the filter thoroughly. It can be hard to remove the dirt completely, and any dirt that remains in the furnace may affect its performance. Reusable filters should be cleaned every three months during heating season. The filter shown here hadn't been changed in two years; the accumulated dust and dirt kept much of the heated air from getting where it was needed.

1

Turn off the furnace. It should be on its own circuit in the breaker panel or fuse box. New installations, like the one shown here, usually have a cutoff mounted right on the furnace.

2

Remove the blower door. In newer furnaces, such as this one, the filter will probably be inside the furnace. On older furnaces the filter may be in the return air vent.

Remove the filter. If it has a cardboard frame, it's a disposable filter. Write down the size of the filter and buy a replacement at a hardware store or home center. If return ducts have filters, inspect them as well.

Vacuum the filter. If the filter has a plastic frame, it is reusable. Vacuum it to remove the larger pieces of dust clogging it. Vacuum the area around the filter, too, to help minimize the particulates that might be drawn into the furnace.

Wash the filter. In the yard, use a hose to rinse the dust out of a reusable filter and the particles from the screen. Allow the filter to dry completely.

Reinstall the filter. Look for markings that indicate which side of the filter should face the fan. Put the filter in place and fasten it—this furnace has a metal hoop that holds it in place. Put the cover back on the furnace.

Insulating Hot-Water Pipes

The pipes that snake out from a hot-water or steam furnace and from the water heater act something like radiators. That is, they put off heat as water or steam passes through them, and the heat typically goes to warming a part of the home that doesn't need it—basements and crawl spaces and the vertical chases in which concealed pipes travel from floor to floor. If you have access to the pipes, you can easily install pipe insulation to slow these heat losses.

Start by measuring the diameter of the pipes that come from the water heater—about 1 inch is common. Then buy foam pipe insulation that has an inside diameter to match.

Safety First

If you have a gas water heater or a boiler, don't use foam pipe insulation near the flue. (Check the nameplate on the equipment for the required clearance from combustible materials.) Instead, substitute unfaced fiberglass pipe wrap, held in place with either foil tape or wire.

1

Cut a miter in the end of a sleeve. Cut a 45-degree angle in one end of the insulation with a pair of scissors.

2

Attach the sleeves. Slip the sleeves over the pipes, placing the miter against the first turn in the pipe.

Cut to length. Cut the sleeves to length with a knife.

Miter the next piece. Cut a 45-degree angle in the sleeve and fit it against the 45-degree angle already in place. Put the sleeve in place and cut or miter it to length.

Continue cutting and fitting. Once you've made the first few turns, the runs of pipe will usually be long and straight. Cover the pipes until they go through the wall or ceiling and are no longer accessible.

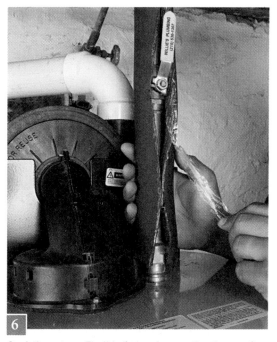

Seal the seam. Flexible foam sleeves, like these, often have adhesive on the edge of the slit so that you can glue the piece together. Remove the protective plastic slip on each side, and push the sides together.

Insulating Furnace Pipes

If you have hot-water heat and the pipes coming out of the boiler are $^3/_4$ inch in diameter or smaller, you can (and should) insulate the pipe the same way you insulate the pipes coming out of a water heater. (See "Insulating Hot-Water Pipes," page 114, for step-by-step directions.) If the pipes are larger, as they often are on older furnaces, you may be able to find foam pipe insulation in the diameter you need; but if not, you'll need to wrap them with either fiberglass or foam tape.

Of the two, foam tape is a bit easier to work with—it's self-adhesive and doesn't require the safety glasses, dust mask, and long sleeves that you need when working with fiberglass. Fiberglass, on the other hand, provides greater R-value and may be worth the extra effort. Each wrap should overlap the previous one by about $^1/_2$ inch, but don't compress the fiberglass as you do it. Compressing fiberglass makes it lose R-value.

Whether you're using fiberglass or foam, the roll is usually too long to handle conveniently. Cut it into manageable lengths, apply a piece, and then start wrapping the next one where the previous one left off.

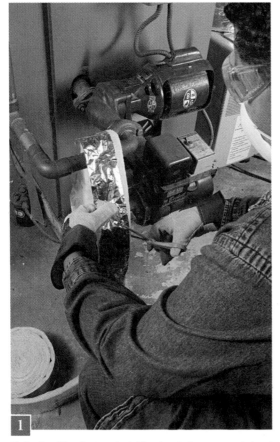

1 **Cut a length of wrapping.** Pipe insulation comes in long rolls, so cut off a piece short enough to work with.

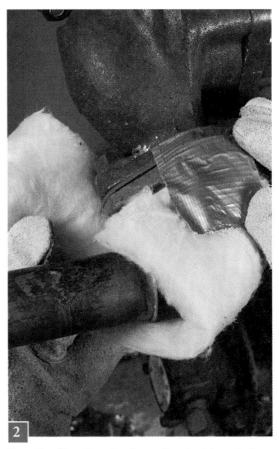

2 **Tape the fiberglass in place.** Use duct tape to tape the fiberglass to the pipe at the end closest the furnace. Some foam pipe wraps are self-adhering; you can skip this step if using them.

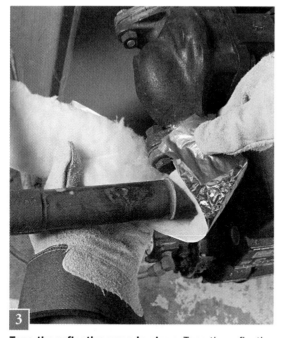

3

Tape the reflective wrap in place. Tape the reflective wrap to the fiberglass—again, this is something you'll skip if you're using foam tape.

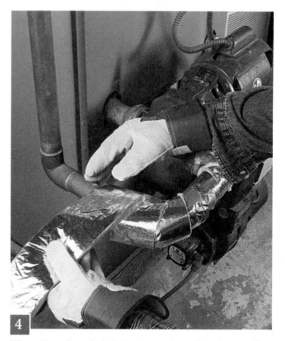

4

Wrap the pipe. Spiral the tape along the pipe so that each turn overlaps the previous turn by $\frac{1}{2}$ inch.

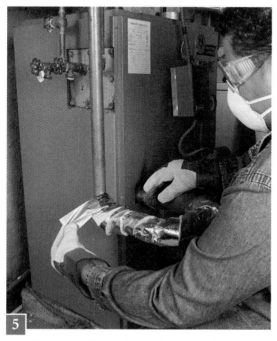

5

Tape the end to the pipe. Continue wrapping until the strip of insulation ends, and then tape it in place. Cut a new piece, tape it in place, and continue along the pipe.

6

Wrap valves and intersections. Wrap valves and intersections in a figure-eight pattern, leaving the valve exposed. Continue wrapping and taping until the pipe passes through the wall or ceiling.

A room with lots of windows to catch the sun can capture enough solar energy to heat itself and even take the chill off a neighboring room.

Heaters for Small Spaces

Space heaters are typically small portable units placed in a room to provide additional heat. Most are compact, so they can be wheeled to wherever needed and then disappear into storage when warm weather returns. Some operate with electricity; others burn kerosene, natural gas, or propane.

In general, space heaters don't save energy. They are best for temporary situations—perhaps an older person who likes a warmer room is visiting. You can also use space heaters to warm a chronically chilly spot, but in the long run you'll save more money by having your home's heating imbalance corrected.

There are three basic types of electric space heaters—baseboard, fan-forced air, and oil-filled. No type is significantly more energy-efficient than the others. The oil-filled type is the quietest (the oil isn't burned; instead it serves to store heat and never needs refilling.) Fan-forced air units heat the space most quickly and keep it at the most constant temperature, but the fan makes them noisy.

Space-Heater Safety

Consider safety when you buy a space heater, particularly a combustion space heater. Unvented kerosene heaters have been banned in some states because they can release nitrogen oxides into the household air. And space heaters are blamed for about 25,000 fires and more than 300 deaths per year in the U.S.

REPAIR OR REPLACE?

The furnace lurks in a seldom-visited corner of the home, and chances are, you pay little attention to it. You pay the bills, get some routine maintenance, and then one chilly winter day, the furnace goes cold.

If it has been reasonably trustworthy and not too costly to run, you may not want to rush to replace it. You should consider replacing the unit if it's more than 15 years old, especially if it has been plagued with repairs. Also lean in favor of jettisoning a coal furnace that was converted to oil or gas.

You May Not Need a New Furnace After All

Don't jump to the conclusion that a poorly performing furnace is giving up the ghost. Here are a few simple procedures that may restore it to good health:

- If the flow from vents is feeble, make sure that the furnace's air filter is free of dirt and dust.

- Check the brains of the system: The thermostat may be suffering from loose wires or a dead battery.

- Look at the fuse for the fan and the circuit breaker(s) serving the furnace.

A space heater is a good way to warm up a chilly spot in the house—temporarily. In the long run, you'll save more money by having a technician fix whatever is keeping heat from getting to where you want it.

■ Still no luck? Then call a repair person before shopping for a furnace. You'll probably get off more cheaply if you fix what you have than buying a replacement—unless a major component such as the heat exchanger or control module is shot. In that case, the furnace may be beyond saving.

BUYING A NEW HEATING SYSTEM

A sparkling new furnace probably is not at the top of your list of dream home improvements. The things just aren't that attractive, and they seem to be among the few products that no one collects or trades on eBay. Nevertheless, this is one big household purchase that really can be called an investment because of the potential energy savings. And with a dependable system at the heart of your home, you will enjoy the intangibles of more comfort and greater peace of mind.

Systems Analysis

Typically, homes are heated by either furnaces or boilers. Furnaces heat air and distribute it through ducts; boilers heat water and send it through pipes, either as steam or as hot water. The efficiency of both systems is indicated as a single Annualized Fuel Utilization Efficiency (AFUE) figure. That sounds straightforward enough, but the greater the efficiency, the more expensive the equipment. A peak-performing unit is likely to have a sure payoff only where winters are very cold. In a more moderate climate, a less-efficient unit may be a sounder investment.

Buying a Gas Furnace

To get the most energy-efficient model, and save the most, look for furnaces with the Energy Star logo. That identifies models with an AFUE rating of at least 90 percent. Energy Star units are about 15 percent more efficient on average than standard models.

Calculate Your Savings

For information on how much different furnace efficiencies might save you, go to *www.Consumer Reports.org/energy*, and click on Calculate Your Savings.

ConsumerReports-org/**energy**

" *To get the most energy-efficient model, and save the most, look for furnaces with the Energy Star logo.* "

Furnace Features Explained

Furnaces come plain and fancy, with features you may or may not care to pay for. The extras are more likely to be found on higher-efficiency furnaces, while some manufacturers also offer them on premium versions of low-efficiency models.

Variable-speed blowers can deliver air more slowly and often more quietly when less heat is needed. Heat can then be delivered more continuously, with fewer uncomfortable drafts or swings in temperature.

Variable heat output can further increase efficiency and comfort by automatically ensuring an even delivery of heat.

Intermittent, direct-spark, and hot-surface ignition make it unnecessary to have a pilot light, with its continuous use of fuel. That increases efficiency and is usually reflected in such furnaces' high AFUE ratings.

Longer warranties typically come with the premium models.

Secondary heat exchangers draw more heat from the burned gas.

Sophisticated air filtration, such as an electrostatic filter or high-efficiency particulate air (HEPA) filter, can reduce the amount of dust that is blown through the heating system. People with asthma or other chronic lung diseases may find some relief, although there's little evidence that others benefit from special filters.

Zoned heating involves a number of thermostats, a sophisticated central controller, and a series of dampers to distribute different amounts of heating or cooling to the various areas of the home. Zoning is particularly helpful in larger homes, as well as those with rooms that vary a good deal in their heating or cooling requirements. Other heating systems, such as hot-water, can also be zoned.

Furnace and Boiler Shopping

It's crucial to choose a furnace or boiler that's the appropriate size for your home. Contractors tend to specify units that are too large, especially for homes that are well-sealed and insulated. But too big a furnace won't keep you cozier; it may just waste fuel because it has to cycle on and off more frequently. The components will tend to wear out faster, as well. Go with a contractor who is willing to accurately calculate your heating needs based on the home's size, design, and construction. A professional heat-loss calculation will include window area and type as well as insulation values throughout the home. Square footage alone is not sufficient information for sizing any heating equipment. The standard computation tool in use today by heating professionals is Manual J, Residential Load Calculation Procedure, published by Air Conditioning Contractors of America (ACCA).

> *A professional heat-loss calculation will include window area and type as well as insulation values throughout the home.*

Even this dependable old basement beast—which started out as a coal furnace and was converted to oil—may be in line for replacement. New furnaces are remarkably more efficient and can earn back their purchase price over time.

Compared with older furnaces, the exhaust from new gas furnaces is a very low temperature—barely enough to warm your hands in some cases. These low-temperature gases are vented to the outside through an special exhaust pipe, rather than a chimney. There's a separate air-intake vent that pulls air from outside for combustion.

If you replace an older gas furnace with one that has an AFUE of 90 percent or more, you'll need to consider the expense of installing vents that meet the requirements of a high-efficiency unit. Also, if other appliances shared a vent or chimney with the existing furnace, they may need new or improved venting as well. Those modifications can add hundreds of dollars to the cost of buying and installing a new furnace.

Working with a Contractor

Then there's the matter of durability. CONSUMER REPORTS has learned from contractors that highly efficient gas furnaces may require more service calls. If you are considering one of those units, ask the contractor about their reliability. Also, have the contractor recommend models with a range of efficiencies and then calculate the annual estimated operating cost of each. Make sure that those estimates include the cost of any changes that need to be made to the home's chimney.

As you can see, the contractor should be very involved in your decision process. To find someone you can trust, ask friends, co-workers, and your local gas utility for their recommendations. Ideally, you should go through this process sometime other than during the heating season. This will allow you more time to select a contractor and arrive at a good price. And you're apt to find that contractors can be more helpful when they aren't hassled by a backlog of emergency no-heat calls.

Going with Gas

While oil furnaces still are common in areas without natural-gas supply lines, natural gas is now used in more than half of American homes. A far smaller number are heated with propane, a gas that is compressed to a liquid for ease of storage and handling, then delivered to the home by truck. Propane is the more expensive of these two nonrenewable gases. But natural gas is delivered by pipelines, and many homes in rural areas are beyond the reach of distribution networks. When a line is extended to a potential customer, a certified technician may be able to convert a propane furnace or boiler to burn natural gas.

All manufacturers offer furnaces in a range of capacities and efficiencies, and CONSUMER REPORTS thinks manufacturers generally deliver on those specifications. Each brand offers a generally similar array of features. That means that rather than concerning yourself with brands, you should concentrate on whether the unit's specifications will meet your needs. From there, it's up to you to see that the furnace is maintained regularly. In a CONSUMER REPORTS survey of hundreds of heating and AC contractors, most said that the main reason for service calls was human error—including inadequate maintenance and improper installation—rather than defective equipment.

Gas furnaces are now considerably more energy-efficient than they were 50 years ago. While a typical furnace made in the late 1950s would have an AFUE rating of about 65 percent, the lowest efficiency now allowed for new units is 78 percent. The most efficient models you can buy have an AFUE of about 97 percent—or near-total efficiency.

Generally speaking, greater fuel efficiency comes at a price. A furnace with a 90 percent

Fuel-Cost-Comparison Calculator

Find out if you could be keeping warm for less with this online computation device. Go to *www.ConsumerReports.org/energy*, click on Fuel Price Comparison, and plug in the variables.

Consumer Reports.org/energy

▦ ▦ ▦ Remodel Radiantly?

In radiant heating, the heat source is embedded in floors (most commonly), or walls, or ceilings. The room's own surfaces act as radiators. Heat radiates directly to the objects—and people—in the room, and it feels like the warmth of the sun rather than a draft of heated air. Because this form of heating is built into the surfaces of a room, it can't easily be retrofitted, but you may want to consider radiant heating for an addition or an extensive renovation. You can also use it to supplement heating in a room—for example, to warm the floor for comfort.

AFUE can cost about $1,000 more than a similarly sized unit with an 80 percent AFUE. You should be able to recoup the difference in savings on fuel. But just how long that will take is affected by your climate, your home's insulative envelope, and the going rate for energy fuel.

Buying an Oil Furnace or Boiler

CONSUMER REPORTS has found that increased efficiency is not usually an economically valid reason to buy a new furnace. The payback period has been too long, but that period will shorten as fuel prices rise.

If the furnace needs replacement, investigate your fuel choices. Find out if natural gas is available in your area and consider propane or even

▦ ▦ ▦ A Solar Collector That You Can Live In

An attached sunspace can contribute warmth to the rest of the home. If the sunspace has substantial masonry floors of stone, tile, or cement, some of this free heat will be stored passively and then gradually released to the living space.

an electric heat pump. Refer to the fuel cost comparison calculator box on page 122 to compare the cost of fuels.

Buying a Heat Pump

Look for Energy Star-qualified heat pumps, which are about 20 percent more efficient than standard models. If you now have an older heat pump, a new replacement may be 20 to 50 percent more efficient. Be aware, though, that not all highly efficient heat pumps are qualified by Energy Star.

As you might expect, the more efficient the heat pump, the more it will cost. There are two measures of the efficiency of a heat pump. One is the Seasonal Energy Efficiency Rating (SEER), which measures the efficiency of the unit during the entire cooling season. The higher the SEER, the higher the efficiency. The other number to look for is the Heating Season Performance Factor (HSPF)—again the higher the number, the better. When weighing the importance of these numbers, consider whether you will use the heat pump more for heating or more for cooling.

Air-source heat pumps are the most common type. Energy Star units will have a SEER of at least 12. Efficiency suffers as outdoor temperatures drop, and typically air-source units are used where winters are moderate.

Geothermal heat pumps can be used in colder areas, taking advantage of the seasonally constant temperatures of the ground or ground water. They are more expensive to install than air-source heat pumps but can be from 30 to 60 percent more

---

Ditch Natural Gas for a Heat Pump?

To get an idea of whether you'd save by switching from natural gas to a heat pump, go to *www.ConsumerReports.org/energy* and click on Natural Gas vs. Heat Pump.

ConsumerReports.org/energy

efficient. Those savings can offset the added cost over a period of 5 to 10 years. Energy Star-qualified geothermals have a SEER of at least 13.

Beware of Things That Go Cold in the Night

A CONSUMER REPORTS survey of more than 36,000 homeowners with gas furnaces reveals that some brands hold up substantially better than others. Respondents reported that the vast majority of repairs were caused by a problem with the furnace itself, not with its installation. So you not only have to find a good installer but also choose a dependable brand. For a comparison of manufacturers' products, see "Repair Report Card," at right. Here are the general findings of the survey:

■ Of furnaces installed in the past eight years, about 1 in 6 had needed repair.

■ Nearly 60 percent of these repairs were to furnaces that had failed completely and stopped producing heat.

■ In nearly 40 percent of the cases, the home was left unheated for at least 24 hours.

■ Nearly 40 percent of the repairs cost $150 or more.

Coaxing More Heat from Wood

As a heat source, burning wood is traditional, cozy, pleasantly scented, and lovely to gaze upon. It also can be very inefficient. In cold-weather tests by Canada's Combustion and Carbonization Research Laboratory, most fireplaces created a net loss of heat, putting more of a load on the home's furnace. You can improve the efficiency by installing glass fireplace doors. They allow you to moderate the draft while providing a view of the fire, but standard tempered-glass doors block the transmission of room-warming infrared rays.

> **Repair Report Card**
> For a look at how well furnaces by principal manufacturers are holding up, go to *www.ConsumerReports.org/energy* and click on Furnace Reliability.
>
> **ConsumerReports**.org/energy

" A CONSUMER REPORTS survey of more than 36,000 homeowners with gas furnaces reveals that some brands hold up substantially better than others. "

The sight of a crackling fire warms you—at least psychologically—but it sucks the heated air from your furnace right up the chimney. You can prevent heated air from escaping and also burn wood more efficiently by investing in a sealed fireplace or an advanced-combustion stove.

New advanced-combustion woodstoves are a remarkable improvement. They lower emissions, are 10 to 20 percent more efficient than standard stoves, and use pyro-ceramic windows to deliver radiant heat into the room.

■ ■ ■ Can You Save Money by Burning Wood?

As prices of common fuels go up, burning wood can look attractive if you have a ready supply and don't mind the added work that's involved. But to find out how much (if anything) you'd save with wood, you'll have to do a bit of basic math.

First, you need to find the BTU (British Thermal Unit) measurement, as shown in "Equivalents to a Cord of Wood," at upper right. As an example, assume that you used 600 gallons of No. 2 fuel oil last year at $2 per gallon, for a total cost of $1,200. How would that compare with burning wood at $150 per cord? (A cord measures 4 by 4 by 8 feet, but note that a "cord run" is a single stack of 16-inch logs that is one-third the volume of a true cord. The energy stored in a cord varies with the species; this example uses red oak, with 24.2 million BTUs per cord, rounded down to 24 million BTUs.)

From the chart "Equivalents to a Cord of Wood," you find that those 600 gallons of fuel oil would equal 3.4 cords for the heating season (600 gallons divided by 175 = 3.4 cords).

And that in turn suggests you could heat with wood for just $510, a considerable savings (3.4 cords × $150/cord = $510). But you also have to consider the efficiency with which the wood is burned. Fireplaces and woodstoves traditionally have ranked low in efficiency, although new wood-burning technologies have made considerable improvements. See the chart "Wood-Heat Efficiency," above right.

If your wood stove has an efficiency rating of 80 percent, and a cord is going for $150, here's how much you can expect to spend for wood if you used 600 gallons of fuel oil last year:

3.4 cords divided by 0.80 efficiency = 4.25 cords.

And 4.25 cords at $150 per cord would total $637.50 for the year's heating bill, assuming that you have an efficient catalytic stove—still a considerable savings of $562.50 over the cost of oil for the year.

Equivalents to a Cord of Wood

Type of fuel	To compare energy of 1 cord of wood
Fuel oil (gallons)	Divide by 175
Coal (pounds)	Divide by 1,600
Natural gas (thousand cubic feet, or MCF)	Divide by 28
Propane gas (gallons)	Divide by 220
Electricity (kilowatts)	Divide by 6,500

Wood-Heat Efficiency

Type of unit	Efficiency (%)
Standard fireplace	Up to 10
Fireplace insert	Up to 20
Simple updraft (Franklin) stove	Up to 30
Airtight stove	Up to 60
Catalytic stove	Up to 80
Pellet-fuel stove	Up to 90

Heating-Fuel-Comparison Calculator

If you don't want to do all the math, the U.S. Department of Energy has created a spreadsheet you can use to compare the relative cost of heating with electricity, natural gas, propane, wood, pellets, kerosene, and coal. To find this tool, go to *www.ConsumerReports.org/energy* and click on Calculate Your Savings.

You'll need a copy of your utility bill to complete the sheet. You'll also need to know how many BTUs you can expect to get from the wood species that you're using. To find that information, go to *www.ConsumerReports.org/energy* and click on BTUs per Cord of Wood.

KEEPING COOL

Home heating is a necessity in many regions of the U.S., and even the most rugged of pioneers had their open-hearth fireplaces and six-plate stoves. But using energy to *cool* the air is a relatively recent idea. And in the rush to air-condition every living space and even some city sidewalks, we sometimes overlook the wealth of traditional, commonsense ways of beating the heat.

An Energy-Efficient Landscape

Landscaping can lower your energy costs in a few ways. By strategically planting trees and shrubs on the side of the home that gets the brunt of the western sun, you can keep the house cooler. Come winter, deciduous (broadleaf) trees will lose their leaves, allowing warming sunlight to reach your windows when you need it.

Trees also can cool the home in summer by the process of transpiration: Their leaves release water vapor for a natural sort of air conditioning. Together with the effect of shading, deciduous

■ ■ ■ In the Still of the Night

- To take advantage of natural cooling from open windows, note when and where breezes enter the home as evening comes on.
- Use window or whole-house fans to bring in more cooling air.
- Close doors and windows by day. Use shades, blinds, or awnings to filter sunlight, particularly for west-facing windows in the afternoon.
- Wait until evening to run the dishwasher, washing machine, and dryer. During these cooler hours, your air conditioner won't have to work as hard to offset the heat produced by the appliances. Electricity rates may be lower at that time, as well.
- Switch to compact fluorescent lamps (CFLs). They use less electricity than incandescents, and put off less waste heat.

On a hot day, you'd stay cool under a tree. Use the same logic when landscaping, placing trees so that they cast a welcome shadow when the western sun is at its most relentless.

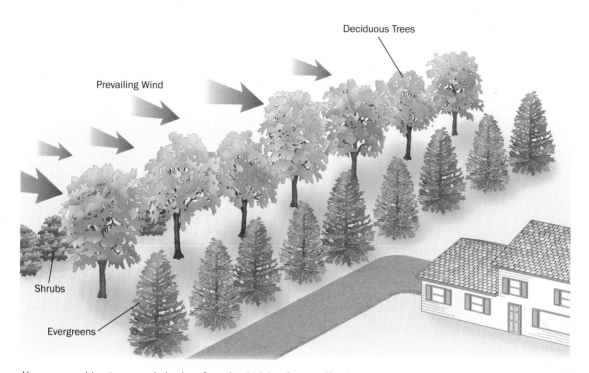

You can combine trees and shrubs of varying heights for an effective barrier to prevailing winds.

trees may lower surrounding air temperatures by enough that you might not feel the need to turn on the air conditioning on some summer days. But before going out in the yard and digging holes for new trees, be sure to observe where shadows fall at various times of the year. Shadows are longest in winter months, and an evergreen tree growing some distance away may block the sun's warming rays.

Trees can help keep the home warmer, too. Windbreaks are a traditional way of protecting homes from chilling winds. And you don't need a towering wall of pines planted a few feet away. A windbreak can be effective as far away as 30 times its height. Ideally, place the trees at a distance from the house equal to two to five times their height, arranging them on the side of the home that catches prevailing winter winds. Rather than plant a row of the same species with mathematical precision, consider an informal grouping of trees and shrubs. The result will look natural, and its mix of heights will do a better job of blocking the wind.

Made in the Shade

You can reduce the energy spent on cooling by using plantings to shade the outside component of the AC system.

Of course a skinny sapling will need years before leafing out into a tree of useful size for climate control. You can expect a tree to begin shading the roof of your home in 5 to 10 years, depending on how large it was when planted, the species you've chosen, and growing conditions.

You don't have to shade the house from top to bottom in order to get a noticeable benefit. Shorter plants can do their part as well. Arrange shrubs so that they will cast shade on patios and other gathering places that tend to become uncomfortably hot. Foundation plantings can shade lower walls and windows, but keep their mature size in mind when setting them out. As they grow, they may create a humid zone that causes paint to peel and wood siding and trim to rot. You'll probably have to add pruning to your annual yard chores to prevent shrubbery from blocking air circulation.

Put a Lid on Unwanted Solar Heat

A dark roof makes an excellent solar collector—just what you don't want in summer if a chronically hot attic is radiating heat into the sweltering bedrooms below. On a sunny day, roofing can heat up to 150° to 190° F. If you live in a warm, sunny climate, you can save on your cooling costs by using light-colored roofing.

FANS: GENERATE YOUR OWN WIND-CHILL FACTOR

Placing fans in strategic places around the house can go a long way toward making you feel cooler without turning down the AC. That means saving energy, because fans draw so much less current than even window air-conditioning units.

The summertime partner to a portable space heater is a freestanding fan. Put it where you want it, and you'll be able to rely less on energy-intensive air conditioning.

Fans work in a couple of ways. Most obviously, they create a breeze that promotes the body's own natural evaporative cooling. It's the summertime version of winter's wind-chill factor. A fan also can be used both to draw in cool outside air and to exhaust hot indoor air, by either placing a fan in a

A freestanding fan can be placed anywhere in the house to create a cooling breeze where there is none. Using a fan instead of an air conditioner is a good way to keep your energy costs down.

■ ■ ■ Fans Cool for Less

Here's a look at the relative costs of cooling options. (These figures compare a whole-house fan that has a $\frac{1}{4}$-hp or $\frac{1}{2}$-hp motor; a fairly large 18,000-BTU/hour window unit; and a 2-ton central-air system. They are calculated for Atlanta, with electricity at 8.5 cents per kilowatt-hour.)

A whole-house fan costs $150 to $350 to buy and runs for 1 to 5 cents per hour.

A window AC costs $250 to $750 to buy and runs for 17 cents per hour.

A central-air system costs $2,000 to $4,000 to buy and install, and runs for 20 cents per hour.

window or permanently installing a whole-house model. Timing is crucial here. You have to pay attention to the temperature—and the relative humidity—of the air within and without your four walls. This exchange of air works only when the outside air feels more comfortable than the air inside the house. Typically, fans are used to exchange the air after sundown and until the world begins to heat up again after dawn.

According to the Florida Solar Energy Center, the cooling effect of a ceiling fan can cut energy use by 14 percent. But that's only if you remember to turn up the AC thermostat when turning on

■ ■ ■ Timely Cooling

You may find it more convenient to operate a whole-house fan with a timer, set to turn the fan on when temperatures drop in the evening, then off before the outdoor air heats up.

"Window fans are inexpensive, easy to install, and cheap to run. A twin-fan model takes better advantage of a limited window opening."

fans. Otherwise, you may be operating both at the same time, an unnecessary expense.

Freestanding Fans

A small, portable interior fan is especially efficient because it can be moved to any hot spot in the home—the kitchen while you're baking cookies in the oven, perhaps, or where you're playing the piano in a patch of sunlight. It can be used in summer to help distribute cooling air from an air conditioner, and to do the same with warm air from registers and radiators in winter.

Window Fans

Window fans are inexpensive, easy to install, and cheap to run. A twin-fan model takes better advantage of a limited window opening. You can use them to supplement cooling breezes, particularly after sundown. Try having a fan blowing in on the ground floor, and a fan blowing out on a floor above. This will boost the "chimney effect" by which warm air rises and vents naturally from the home. There are even designs that allow you to close the sash without removing the fan, so that you can shut out the rain or make the home more secure while you're away. When cooler weather returns in the fall, you can slip these fans into plastic garbage bags and store them out of sight—not so easily accomplished with a bulky window AC.

Whole-House Fans

In the summer, a whole-house fan can do the work of an air conditioner for about one-tenth the electricity. To take advantage of cool night air, a thermostatically controlled fan will turn on in the evening and off in the early morning. It exhausts hot attic air, and draws in outside air from open windows throughout the house. The fan often is installed in an upstairs hallway and typically has louvers that automatically close to contain the household's cool air. Ask a contractor for advice on the appropriate size for your home. At night, a whole-house fan can lower household temperatures by 3° to 6° F. One caution though: If you predominately cool with air conditioning, don't switch to fan ventilation for cooling on humid nights, even if it is cool outside. The moisture that will enter your home will take additional cooling energy to remove the next day.

A whole-house fan pulls cool evening air in from outside the house, cooling the house without the expense of air conditioning at a time when most people are home.

Attic Fans

An attic fan has a different role than a whole-house unit. Where a whole house fan pulls cool air into the entire house, an attic fan is intended to remove excess heat from the attic. An attic fan can be controlled by a thermostat, so that it goes on automatically when temperatures climb to a certain point. Attic entrances should be well-sealed to prevent drawing cooled air up from the living space below. It is also important to provide adequate air intake, usually in the form of vents in the roof overhangs, so the fan can work efficiently, using as little electricity as possible. With adequate intake, the cost of running the fan is about equal to the money saved, because your air conditioner doesn't have to fight the heat radiating from the attic. An attic fan is usually necessary only to compensate for poorly designed attic ventilation.

Ceiling Fans

A ceiling fan can be a quiet, cooling presence in the home. With its gentle breeze, you may find that you can nudge up the AC thermostat by about 4° F. That means if you're using air conditioning along with your fan, you can set the thermostat at a higher-than-normal temperature to save energy.

> " *At night, a whole-house fan can lower household temperatures by 3° to 6° F.* "

The average ceiling fan uses about as much electricity as a 100-watt lightbulb, so you can run one for just pennies a day. Most ceiling fans can be switched to operate in reverse. The idea is that the fan will draw warm air toward the ceiling and circulate it back down into the living area of the room. While this does happen, CONSUMER REPORTS tests have found that in most cases the draft created by the fan made room occupants uncomfortable.

When installing ceiling fans, try to locate them as close as possible to seating areas— you may want to install more than one fan in a room. Ceiling fans often have a built-in light, or a separate kit that enables you to add a light. Either way, a light is a good idea, especially since installation is easiest if you use the fan to replace a ceiling light. The fan's light and the speed and direction of the fan can be adjusted with a remote control on many fans, which simplifies wiring.

When purchasing fans, consider buying the largest ones possible— you'll be able to run them on lower speeds, which will minimize noise. Also, when shopping for a fan, be aware that the costlier models tend to operate more quietly, but you should check the noise level as stated in sones. A rating of 1.5 sones means that the fan will operate quietly, but you may want to consider models that are as low as 1.0 or 0.5 sones. Finally, if the fan weighs less than 35 pounds, you can usually hang it from an outlet box marked for a load capacity that's at least equal to the fan's weight. Otherwise, additional support, like that shown in "Installing a Ceiling Fan," page 132, is required. Be sure to check your fan's directions to make sure you're using adequate support.

A ceiling fan can save energy and increase your comfort in the summer. It creates a cooling breeze, lessening the need for air conditioning.

Installing a Ceiling Fan

A ceiling fan typically is installed where there is an existing ceiling light. There's no additional wiring unless you'd like the fan light on a separate switch instead of a pull chain. If you want a separate switch, or want to put a fan where there's no existing light fixture, have an electrician do the wiring for you.

Before you buy the fan, make sure that the blades will clear the floor by a minimum of 7 feet—more if you have very tall family or friends. Specific installation steps vary from one manufacturer to another; closely follow the directions that come with the fan.

Part of the installation will probably involve removing the old junction box in the ceiling and replacing it with something designed to hold the weight of the fan. The box will probably need bracing, too. The expandable metal brace shown here provides plenty of strength and is easy to install.

The wiring for the installation shown here is typical for a ceiling fan and light that operate on a single wall switch. (You can turn the light on and off with a pull chain or a remote control.) If you want separate switches, check the directions that come with the fan.

1

Shut off the power. Cut power to the ceiling fixture at the circuit breaker panel or fuse box. Remove the screws that hold the fixture in place. Remove the plastic nuts that hold the wires together by turning and pulling gently on the nuts. Use tape to identify which wires were connected to the fixture and which, if any, will need to be reconnected to each other.

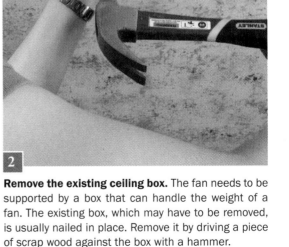

2

Remove the existing ceiling box. The fan needs to be supported by a box that can handle the weight of a fan. The existing box, which may have to be removed, is usually nailed in place. Remove it by driving a piece of scrap wood against the box with a hammer.

Replace the existing ceiling box with a fan box. Ask at the store for the proper box. Often, you'll need to use an expanding metal ceiling-fan hanger bar to support the box. Put the bar through the opening in the ceiling, and rest the end supports on the ceiling.

Turn the hanger bar. Turn the bar to make the threaded rod in it travel toward the ceiling joists. Once it contacts the joists, turn the bar with a wrench to seat it firmly.

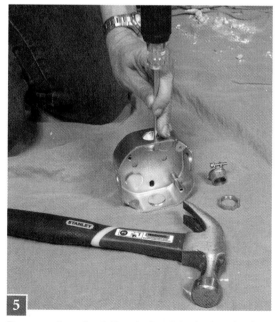

Remove a knockout. To get wires into the junction box, you need to make an opening. Strike one of the knockouts with a screwdriver and hammer, and enlarge the opening with a screwdriver. Remove the disk with pliers.

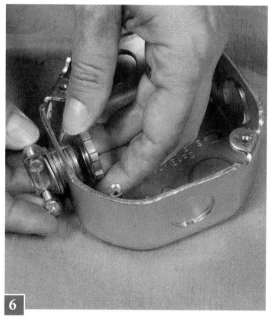

Install a cable clamp. Cable clamps are required by code and are meant to protect the wiring from the sharp edges of the junction box. Put the clamp through the opening, and thread on the nut that comes with it.

Hang the box. Attach the fan's mounting bracket to the bar, pull the wires through the cable clamp, put the box on the bracket, and thread on nuts to hold the assembly together.

Install a medallion. If the ceiling is damaged—or if you damaged it during the installation—you can cover the damage with a plastic medallion that will look like plaster once it is painted. Put some construction adhesive on the medallion, and put it in place.

Install the mounting bracket. The fan will come with a hanging bracket that goes on the junction box. Attach it as directed by the manufacturer.

Attach the fan to the bracket. The fan will require some assembly. Follow the manufacturer's directions, and then position the fan on the bracket. The bracket on this fan, like most brackets, allows you to hang the fan temporarily so you can work on the wiring.

Wire the fan. Twist the two black wires together, the two white wires together, and the two green wires together. Cover with plastic wire nuts, and wrap the nuts and wires with electrical tape to further hold the nuts in place.

Hang the fan. Put the fan in place, and screw the fan to the mounting bracket as directed by the manufacturer.

Attach the fan blades. Once the fan is in place, screw the blades to it, following the directions that came with the fan.

Attach the light. If your fan has a light fixture, wire it as directed, put the bulb in place, and attach it to the fan.

CENTRAL AIR

Sometimes it just isn't enough to move air around in order to get comfortable. Air conditioning, once something of a luxury and found only in some homes, is now a standard feature across the country. AC units really spin the electric meter, but both room-sized air conditioners and central-air systems have become far more efficient in recent years.

Central air conditioning tempers the heat and humidity of summer with just a background whisper of moving air. But it comes at a cost. Central air is typically the main user of electricity in the home, drawing more power in just a few warm-weather months than the refrigerator does in a full year. (To estimate just how much you pay for cooling, do a bit of arithmetic: Find the difference between electric bills in a month when you don't need the AC and those in a month when it is used the most.)

Central-AC Maintenance

Central air-conditioning systems tend to be out of sight and out of mind. Aside from calling in a service person for an annual inspection, there are a few straightforward ways you can help keep cooling costs down and extend the life of the system.

Clean or replace the filters monthly during the cooling season. They usually are located in the return-duct grille, and also may be found in the unit itself. Filters help to keep the air conditioner's coils from building up a coat of dust that acts as an insulative coat, reducing efficiency. Even if the filters get proper attention, the evaporator will eventually become dirty, and it should be checked annually and cleaned when needed.

Inspect the outdoor condenser coils for the debris that is apt to be drawn into the unit. To help keep the air conditioner clean, keep vegetation at least 2 feet away, and do what you can to prevent leaves, grass clippings, lawn chemicals such as

Evaporative Coolers

In warm, arid parts of the country, an evaporative (or "swamp") cooler can lower household temperatures using fewer kilowatts than an air conditioner uses. You may have seen campers' canteens with a canvas cover that can be saturated with water for an evaporative cooling effect. These evaporative home coolers work in the same way, drawing warm outside air over wet pads. As the water evaporates, the air is cooled—less dramatically than with an AC, but often enough to make rooms comfortable. A large cooler, sized for the entire home, can lower temperatures from 15° to 40° F, while using just a third or so of the electricity needed to run an AC unit.

The initial cost of an evaporative cooler is only about half that of AC. And while an air conditioner typically circulates the same indoor air, a cooler brings in a continuous fresh supply. The air is either delivered to a central part of the home or distributed through the existing ductwork. For cooling on a smaller scale, you can buy window units that will lower the temperature of a room by 5° to 15° F. Coolers aren't a good choice in humid regions, because their evaporative effect is lessened, and they also raise the humidity of the air that they process.

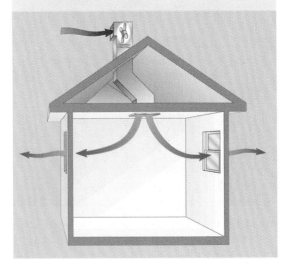

> *All sorts of variables about your home and climate have to be taken into consideration.*

fertilizer, and lint from a dryer vent from ending up in the coils. Those things can block airflow and cause corrosion. The thin, foil-like aluminum fins on evaporator and condenser coils are easily bent, reducing their effectiveness. Air-conditioning dealers sell a special comb for realigning them.

Buying a New Central AC

Energy costs can be expected to continue climbing, and it may make sense to replace the entire cooling system if your current AC is prone to problems. Replacing just the condenser (the outdoor component) can result in compromised efficiency. To be sure of benefiting from the most-efficient technology available today, you'll also have to replace the cooling coil attached to your furnace or packaged indoor blower coil.

It's necessary to get the size right when buying a central AC. That doesn't refer to how large the thing looks but to its cooling capacity. If the system is too big, it can be noisy and will tend to rapidly cycle on and off, shortening its useful life. If the system is too small, there may be insufficient airflow and cooling, which can also wear out mechanical components. Sizing doesn't just concern the AC unit itself. The contractor will need to check the size and condition of the home's air ducts, sealing them as necessary and perhaps adding new ductwork and registers.

All sorts of variables about your home and climate have to be taken into consideration. An HVAC contractor can determine the appropriate size by feeding this data into a program such as the Residential Load Calculation Procedure; see "Cool Savings," right, for more on this.

Once you know the size needed for your home, turn your attention to the Seasonal Energy

An air conditioner has to rid itself of the heat that it draws from the house, and that means you'll need to make sure that the outside of the unit hasn't become crowded by overgrown vegetation.

Cool Savings

For information on how much you might save with a more-efficient air conditioner, go to *www.ConsumerReports.org/energy* and click on Central Air Cost Calculator. This will take you to an energy-saving site where you'll click on the central-air-conditioner link to download the calculator.

ConsumerReports.org/energy

Efficiency Ratio (SEER). If you have an older system with a SEER rating of 6 or less, replacing it with current model can cut your air conditioning costs in half. Federal regulations now require manufacturers to produce central air conditioners with an efficiency of at least 13 SEER, but this doesn't mean the system that an installer offers you will be rated that high. Less-efficient systems may still be on the market, so check the yellow EnergyGuide label before you seal the deal.

ROOM AIR CONDITIONERS

If you need to cool only a couple of rooms—bedrooms, perhaps, or an office in the attic—window-mounted air conditioners will cost a lot less to purchase and operate than a whole-house system. Most room-sized ACs are intended for double-hung windows, but you also can find models designed for casement or slider windows. Some are designed for in-wall installation. There even are freestanding models that can be wheeled from room to room as needed, with an exhaust hose that goes out a window. Tests by CONSUMER REPORTS have found that these portable air conditioners are noisy and that they deliver only about half of the cooling that they claim.

To get the most from a room air conditioner, try to install it on the north or east side of the house, where it will escape the brunt of the summer sun's heat. (The afternoon sun is often said to be worse, heating up the house and the air conditioner at the hottest time of day.) And while shade will help the AC perform better, vegetation should be kept at least 2 feet away to allow air to circulate freely around it. And before taking the trouble to hoist the thing into a window, be sure that the room's circuit has sufficient amperage. The owner's manual should specify the necessary amp rating for the circuit breaker or fuse.

Some units have an energy-saver switch. This cycles both the fan and the compressor on and off. With today's common electronic controls, they typically do maintain an even temperature while also efficiently removing moisture from the air. However, CR finds that the sudden noise change when going on and off can be very disturbing for sleep. Further, the energy advantage is minimal. Another feature you might see is the "vent." While there are those that intake fresh air and others that exhaust stale air (and some with both), CONSUMER REPORTS found that the air exchange is so small that it is ineffective.

> *To get the most from a room air conditioner, try to install it on the north or east side of the house, where it will escape the brunt of the summer sun's heat.*

Of course, the cheapest mode of operation is to turn the AC off. When the outdoor air turns cooler, you should shut off the AC and rely on natural breezes to do the cooling. In fact, an air conditioner may not operate well if outdoor temperatures drop to 60° F or below. You also can lessen the load on an air conditioner simply by closing the door to adjacent spaces that don't need cooling. Also, if you won't be using the room for several hours, turn off the unit, set its thermostat higher, or use the 24-hour timer to set an on-off cycle that suits your daily living pattern.

Buying a New Room AC

When it comes time to replace an old room AC, keep in mind that the new units can reduce your cooling costs by 25 percent or more. Don't buy an air conditioner that's too large for the space it will be cooling on the theory that it'll keep you more comfortable—the reverse is true. An oversized unit

---

Sizing and Choosing a Room AC

You should consider two things when picking a room air conditioner: You want to get the most efficient model, and you want to get one the right size. For the latest Ratings of room air conditioners, go to *www.ConsumerReports.org/energy* and click on Efficient Air Conditioners.

To help you choose the right size, the following site allows you to plug in facts about the area to be cooled. Go to *www.ConsumerReports.org/energy* and click on Sizing a Room Air Conditioner.

ConsumerReports.org/energy

will cool things off quickly but then shut off before it has had a chance to lower the humidity to a comfortable level. The result is a cold and damp room. To avoid ending up with a bigger air conditioner than you need, you need to determine the proper cooling capacity—the amount of heat and moisture that the model can transfer from indoor air to the outdoors.

After you've found out the best cooling capacity for your situation, shop around for an AC of that size with good efficiency numbers. The higher the EER (Energy Efficiency Rating), the more efficient the AC. (EER, which is used to measure window air conditioners, is a measure of the unit's efficiency at a steady state, as opposed to SEER, which averages efficiency over the entire cooling season.) Shop for an air conditioner with an EER of at least 10.

If you haven't bought an air conditioner in a while, don't be surprised by the big new plug, which is designed to help prevent fires. The plug shuts down power when it senses that the air conditioner cord is damaged. The new plugs are known by different names, including leakage-current-detection-interrupters (LCDI) and arc shields. They have test and reset buttons like those on bathroom and outdoor outlets.

Maintaining a Window AC

To clean the filter, remove the interior grille or simply slide the filter frame out of its slot, depending on the design of the unit. Wash the filter gently in warm, soapy water and rinse well. Allow it to dry, then reinstall it.

Ensure that outdoor louvers and coil surfaces are free of debris. You can rinse the unit with a hose or blow it off with a yard blower or vacuum. Before reinstalling the air conditioner, seal around its perimeter with new weatherstripping.

Dehumidifiers

In many parts of the country, keeping comfortable involves reducing the relative humidity. An air con-

Some units have a slide-out chassis, which provides you access to debris that can build up inside the cabinet of your air conditioner and cut down its efficiency. Vacuum every now and then to keep it in top running shape.

ditioner performs this function while cooling the air. But if you don't want the cooling, a dehumidifier will do the job. Before buying a unit for a clammy basement, try taking preventative measures instead. Make sure the clothes dryer is properly vented to the outside; take care of any leaky outdoor faucets; and extend downspouts that aren't carrying rainwater far enough from the foundation.

Dehumidifiers are a variation on air conditioners. As humid air is blown over cold, refrigerant-filled coils, moisture condenses and drips into a tank or through a hose to a drain. This air is then blown across the condenser coil, which heats it, thus lowering its relative humidity. Operating a dehumidifier will tend to raise the temperature of the room it resides in because the electric energy it consumes is converted to heat.

If you don't plan to connect your dehumidifier to a hose for continuous draining, buy a model with a good-sized tank so you won't have to empty the condensed water as often. CONSUMER REPORTS recommends spending a bit more for a large-capacity dehumidifier; it will operate faster and more efficiently than smaller units.

Dehumidifier Maintenance

At the heart of a dehumidifier are the cold coils that cool the air, causing airborne moisture to condense and collect in a removable container or drain out through a hose. Both the coils and the container bear watching.

If operated in a cold room, such as a basement, where the temperature might dip into the 60s or 50s, dehumidifiers will sometimes get so cool that ice forms on them. Check the coils daily during cool weather to make sure they aren't icing up. Turn the machine off if they do. Some models with electronic controls claim to be suitable for cold-temperature operation. They control the compressor operation to prevent ice formation on the coil.

On the water-collection front, mold can form in the collection tank. Controlling the mold may not affect energy efficiency, but it affects your health. If mold forms in the dehumidifier, it may be broadcast into the home to cause itchy eyes and breathing troubles. Wash the tank in soap and water regularly.

As shown here, you should also clean and, in some cases, oil the dehumidifier to keep it in top running order.

Dehumidifier Recommendations

When shopping for a dehumidifier, buy one with the largest capacity you can afford. Look for a model with a large water reservoir or a hose connection. You also want to make sure that the model has a separate on/off switch.

Energy Star models are assigned an energy factor in terms of liters per kilowatt hour—the higher the number, the more efficient the dehumidifer. To find a listing of Energy Star models, go to *www.ConsumerReports.org/energy* and click on Dehumidifer Models. This will take you to the Energy Star Web site, where you can click on Product List.

ConsumerReports.org/energy

1 **Remove the front and back.** Unplug the dehumidifier before working on it. In most cases you'll be able to get inside the back of the machine easily. Getting to the inner workings for the front may require loosening some screws.

2 **Clean the filter and coils.** Vacuum the filter and condenser coils to remove dust that is interfering with the machine's airflow.

7

FUEL-EFFICIENT DRIVING

Gasoline prices have spiked before, but this time is different. There's now little reason to believe that we will see a long-term return to cheaper gas. And worries about air pollution, carbon-dioxide emissions, and our dependence on imported oil continue to grow.

Meanwhile, according to the Environmental Protection Agency, the average fuel economy of 2005 cars and light trucks was only 21 miles per gallon, the worst it has been in 17 years. That's due to the American penchant for large vehicles. Of course, you don't have to drive a big SUV. The good news is that thanks to advances in automotive technology, there are now cars on the market that get dramatically better gas mileage than was available just a few years ago.

If you're be in the market for a new car, you can look at your options later in this chapter. But if you're not looking to replace your car right now, let's start by looking at ways to squeeze the best possible mileage out of your current vehicle.

GREEN DRIVING

You don't have to invest in cutting-edge technology to get more miles per gallon and pollute less. The simplest approach is to modify your driving habits.

Avoid idle moments. Don't let the engine idle any longer than necessary, whether starting up or sitting in traffic. It is generally more efficient to turn off the engine than to idle for longer than 30 seconds.

Don't tailgate. Curious, but true: Tailgating can reduce your mileage. By keeping a good distance between your vehicle and those ahead, you'll do less braking and accelerating, with a potential benefit of 5 to 10 percent more miles to the gallon.

Use cruise control. Cruise control is more than a convenience. Because it keeps your speed constant, you are apt to use less fuel.

Get the junk out of your trunk. The stuff you store in the trunk may be out of sight and out of mind, but the car still has to lug it around. If this cargo weighs 100 pounds, you're getting 1 to 2 percent fewer miles per gallon.

Lighten up, lead foot. You pay a premium for speed. That's in large part because aerodynamic drag exponentially increases as you drive faster. If you drive at a 65-mile-per-hour clip instead of at 55, your fuel consumption rises by 20 percent. Goose it up to 75 mph, and it rises 25 percent more.

Streamlining. At highway speeds, more than half of a vehicle's power (and fuel) is used to push the

The trunk may be a convenient place to stash all sorts of tools and play equipment, but you pay a price for transporting that added weight.

> *Cruise control is more than a convenience. Because it keeps your speed constant, you are apt to use less fuel.*

car through the air. You can reduce the aerodynamic drag by removing temporary racks and rooftop carriers when they aren't needed.

Combine trips. As an engine warms up, it uses less fuel, creates fewer exhaust emissions, and is less prone to wear. That means short trips are especially costly: The engine spends less time operating optimally. Try to combine errands so that you do more driving while the engine is fully warmed up.

Window air conditioners. You've probably heard this advice: You'll use less gas if you roll up the

windows and use the air conditioning on a hot day. The theory is that open windows mess up the car's aerodynamics. CR's engineers tested this theory and found it to be a myth. They found that the effect on fuel efficiency of opening the windows at 65 mph was not even measurable. On the other hand, while it's true that running the air conditioner requires the engine to work harder, tests with a Toyota Camry at 65 mph showed that mileage dropped by only 1 mile or so per gallon with the AC on. The upshot? Running the air conditioner will lower your mileage, but not by much. It might be well worth the slight added cost if the AC helps you to stay more alert and comfortable.

Have the oxygen sensor checked. If the engine's oxygen sensor needs to be replaced, the repair might increase your mileage by a dramatic 40 percent.

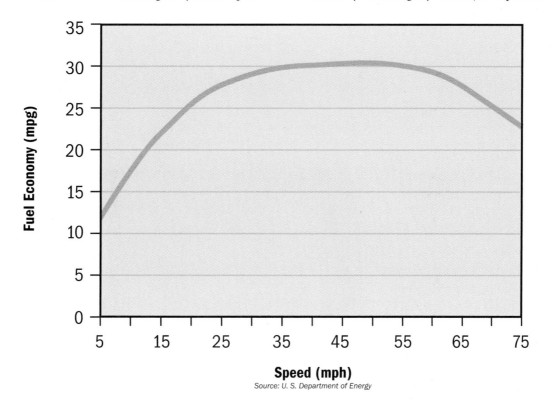

Speed (mph)

Source: U. S. Department of Energy

Do you wince every time the price of gas goes up another dime per gallon? Here's something to remember that can help offset the increase: Your car's gas mileage decreases rapidly at speeds above 60 mph.

Change the oil. It's the job of oil to reduce the friction between the engine's moving parts, which not only extends engine life but also improves efficiency. By changing the oil at the intervals recommended by the vehicle manufacturer, usually every 5,000 to 10,000 miles, you can get more miles per gallon. Use the recommended weight of oil; that alone can make a difference of 1 or 2 percent. If the label says "Energy Conserving" on the American Petroleum Institute (API) performance symbol, the oil has additives that will further minimize friction.

Use regular gas. Most cars are designed to run on regular gasoline. If your owner's manual calls for regular fuel, don't buy premium with the idea that you're doing your engine a favor. Higher-octane gas isn't really better than regular; high-octane formulations are simply less prone to knocking than lower octanes. Even if you have a car for which premium is recommended, you can often run it on regular gas. That's because they have a knock-sensor system that automatically adjusts the timing to eliminate the knock when a lower-octane gas is used. The one sacrifice is a slight reduction in power, although CR has found that the differences aren't perceivable during normal driving. If you try running such a car on regular and hear pings or knocks, then try midgrade gas or stick to premium.

A good deal of a vehicle's power goes into pushing through the air. Removing a roof rack can increase your mileage by reducing the aerodynamic drag that it causes.

Don't Bother Buying Gadgets That Claim to Stretch Mileage

Stay away from gizmos that promise better fuel economy. They don't work, according to tests by both CR and the EPA. The Fuel Genie is a plastic gadget with curved blades that is placed inside the air-intake hose to improve airflow. But in CR's tests, there was no significant improvement in performance or fuel economy. The Tornado is a similar device, made of stainless steel, and again neither power nor gas mileage benefited. The Platinum Gas Saver is connected to a vacuum line leading to the intake manifold, supposedly so that microscopic platinum particles from a liquid reservoir will help burn gas more efficiently and cleanly. Once again, CR found no improvement. So, to get the most from a tank of gas, follow your vehicle's service schedule instead of investing in unproven products that make big promises.

" Judging by years of real-world road tests by CR, the EPA's fuel-economy figures are inflated—by as much as 50 percent on some models. "

The Most Fuel-Efficent Car that Meets Your Needs

Whether you are looking for a sedan, an SUV, a truck, or any other category of vehicle, Consumer Reports Online has made it easy to discover which vehicles in your category get the best gas mileage. Go to *www.Consumer Reports.org/energy* and click on Mileage Comparisons. There you will find Ratings for all the cars CR has tested. With a click of your mouse, you can sort the ratings by several criteria, including overall miles per gallon.

ConsumerReports-org/energy

EPA FUEL-ECONOMY FIGURES ARE GREATLY INFLATED

Automakers have been criticized for producing vehicles that get so-so gas mileage. And the situation is worse than it looks. Judging by years of real-world road tests by CR, the EPA's fuel economy figures are inflated—by as much as 50 percent on some models. Shortfalls in mpg occurred in 90 percent of vehicles that CR tested, and included most makes and models. Overall, the gas-powered vehicles that CR studied delivered 9 percent fewer mpg on average than their EPA stickers claimed. While it is true that hybids and diesels are thriftier in their use of fuel than are cars with conventional gas engines, the difference isn't as great as EPA fuel-economy figures would make you think. Diesel and hybrid cars averaged 18 mpg less in CR real-world driving tests than the EPA fuel economy displayed on their stickers.

The discrepancy between CR and EPA estimates can be attributed to an antiquated EPA test that is done on a stationary machine and doesn't take into consideration how driving conditions have changed. For example, the EPA tests highway driving at an average of 48.5 mph and a maximum

Save Money and Spare the Atmosphere

Carbon dioxide is considered a major contributor to global warming, and one-fourth of the CO_2 generated in the U.S. comes from motor vehicles. If you switch from a car that gets 15 mpg to one that gets 30, you'll be contributing about 3.75 tons less CO_2 per year to the atmosphere—and saving hundreds of dollars in fuel costs along the way.

■■ Miles-per-Gallon Milestones

1975. Passenger cars got only 14 mpg on average, and light trucks just 10.5. The federal government enacted fuel-economy requirements that year in response to the 1973 Arab oil embargo, which sparked fuel shortages and sent gas prices skyrocketing. The requirements, known as Corporate Average Fuel Economy (or CAFE, pronounced café) standards, are national goals designed to prod automakers to produce more fuel-thrifty vehicles.

1985. CAFE required the fleet of passenger cars to average 27.5 mpg and light trucks, 19.5. The different standards for cars and trucks can be traced back to the late 1970s, when the auto industry pressured Congress to cut the mileage requirements for light trucks, which included mainly pickup trucks and cargo vans used commercially.

Today. Pickups, SUVs, minivans, and some station wagons (which the EPA considers light trucks) now account for about half of all new vehicles sold. That helps explain why fuel economy has slumped to the level of the late 1980s. Between 1987 and 2005, car and light-truck manufacturers slashed the average 0-60 acceleration time by 24 percent while they bulked up the average vehicle weight by 27 percent. To accomplish this, horsepower is up 89 percent for cars and 99 percent for trucks since 1981.

Tomorrow. If fuel-economy averages could be nudged upward just 7 mpg, by 2011 we could reduce our annual gasoline needs by about 10 billion gallons. To put that into perspective, the U.S. goes through about 250 billion gallons of petroleum a year. For now, the new 2006 CAFE standards include tougher mile-per-gallon goals for manufacturers of SUVs and light trucks, said to potentially result in a savings of 3 billion gallons of gas per year.

> *If fuel-economy averages could be nudged upward just 7 mpg, by 2011 we could reduce our annual gasoline needs by about 10 billion gallons.*

of 60 mph. But the national 55-mph speed limit is history, with some states posting limits as high as 75 mph. CONSUMER REPORTS highway estimates are based on driving 65 mph on a flat section of highway. Drivers also spend much more time in stop-and-go traffic than when the EPA devised its tests.

Cars have changed, as well. Since 1981, horsepower is up 89 percent for cars and 99 percent for trucks. Many more cars now come with automatic transmissions and four-wheel drive, and almost all have air conditioning—all of which burn more gas.

By contrast, CR's fuel economy testing is done on real roads and on its own track using vehicles purchased anonymously from local dealers. Overall fuel economy is judged from city driving, highway driving, and a 150-mile trip of mixed driving.

As of this writing, the EPA had no plan to change its testing method. However, beginning

---

Cheap Gas

Want a site that will help you find the cheapest gas in your area? Go to *www.ConsumerReports. org/energy* and click on Cheap Gas. It will take you to a map of the 50 states, which is linked to another site with up-to-the-moment prices for regular gas. Click on your state and take a look. For example, a North Dakota search found that you couldn't beat the price at the pumps of Flying J in Fargo, though that could change from day to day.

ConsumerReports.org/energy

in 2008 the EPA is planning to change the way it calculates fuel economy in order to be more in line with real-world conditions. The calculation change is expected to reduce the city mileage estimates for most vehicles, starting in the 2008 model year, by 10 to 20 percent. Highway mileage estimates would drop 5 to 15 percent.

GREEN MACHINES

The conventional gas engine wastes most of the fuel you put in the tank. Only about 15 percent of the energy burned goes to propelling the vehicle, lighting the lights, and running the AC. The rest is squandered by the inefficient operation of the engine and drive train, as well as by idling in traffic. A number of promising alternative-fuel vehicles are under development, with some models now on the market.

Hybrid Cars: Two Engines Can Be Better Than One

Hybrid vehicles have made the biggest splash. They team a small gas engine with an electric motor. The systems used in many hybrid models can run on the electric motor, the gasoline engine, or a combination of the two, depending on the driving conditions. A car with a mild hybrid system, such as that used in the Honda Accord Hybrid, uses the electric motor to provide extra power when needed but can't run solely on electric power. Either system can be designed to increase acceleration as well as fuel economy.

Unlike a purely electric car, hybrids generate their own electricity and don't have to be plugged in to recharge their batteries. (See "Save Every Time You Stop," page 148, for more on electric cars.)

Hybrids likely will continue generating consumer interest, too, if gasoline prices remain high. The Toyota Prius and Honda Civic Hybrid

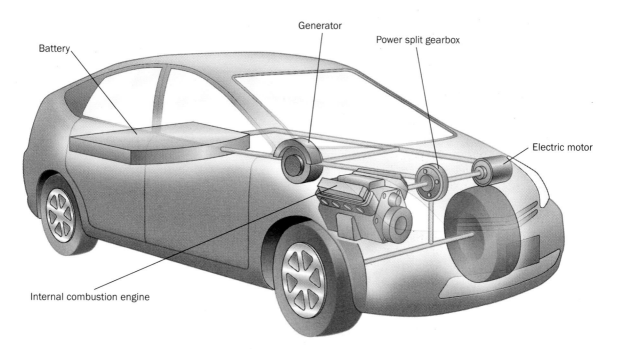

In a full hybrid, a power-split gearbox determines whether an internal combustion engine or an electric motor powers the car. When there is little demand for power, such as at idle speeds, the electric motor does the work. The internal combustion engine powers the car when demand for power is higher. Both motors power the car when accelerating. When coming to a stop, the wheels power the generator, helping to recharge the battery.

delivered an excellent 44 and 37 mpg, respectively, in CONSUMER REPORTS' real-world fuel-economy tests. Beyond the improved mileage figures, hybrids have shown excellent reliability, and owners seem passionate about them, rating them among the best in CR's Annual Car Owner Satisfaction Survey.

Even though hybrids go farther on a gallon of gas, you aren't necessarily assured of a payback. According to CONSUMER REPORTS' analysis, some hybrids may pay off their extra

The Toyota Prius gets the best mileage of any five-seat car tested by CR.

initial cost over a period of five years, provided you can take advantage of tax credits. But with other models, you'd still be out a percentage of the purchase price. Here's CR's rundown of things to consider before buying a hybrid vehicle:

Higher retail price. Hybrids cost more because of their advanced technology and their additional equipment, including two motors and a battery

■ ■ ■   Save Every Time You Stop

Hybrids slow down and stop differently from conventional cars. They use regenerative braking to generate electricity with the energy that is usually wasted as friction when putting on the brakes. The electric motor adds its resistance when braking, and as the motor spins, it acts as a generator to store electricity in the battery until needed. Once the car comes to a stop, the engine automatically shuts off. No idling means no zero-mile-per-gallon time at stoplights. The engine starts up again automatically when needed. A console, shown below, shows fuel consumption and which power unit is working.

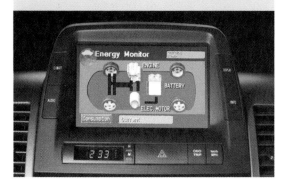

Hybrid Tax Break

While federal tax credits have made it easier to afford a hybrid's higher price, this is a limited-time offer. Once a manufacturer sells 60,000 hybrid vehicles, the credits will be gradually phased out. This total is for all of a manufacturer's hybrid models combined, and not for specific brands. For example, Toyota's total would include both cars with that nameplate and also Lexus. Once the credits are phased out, CR calculates that hybrids will cost an additional $650 to $3,150.

For the latest IRS information on tax incentives for buying a hybrid, go to *www.ConsumerReports.org/energy* and click on Hybrid Tax Break.

pack. Also, some hybrid models come with top-of-the-line trim, extra engine performance, and other added features. If those options aren't important to you, look for a hybrid with fewer options and a lower markup.

Higher maintenance and repair costs. Hybrids operate with expensive battery packs that have a replacement cost estimated at about $3,000 or more. Fortunately, most manufacturers cover hybrid components, including the battery pack, for at least eight years or 80,000 miles. Replacement cost might be a concern if you buy a used hybrid after the warranty has expired. But automakers put the life of these batteries at between 150,000 and 180,000 miles, and as of this writing, they report having to replace only a handful of them.

Scheduled maintenance may cost more. The cost of scheduled maintenance generally is about the same as for conventional vehicles.

You don't have to buy an unusual vehicle to get better mileage. The Honda Pilot (top), with a conventional gas engine, goes substantially farther on a gallon of fuel than the Dodge Durango (bottom).

■ ■ ■ Consider All Your Options

You don't necessarily have to buy a hybrid to conserve gas. There are alternatives. Begin by deciding what type of vehicle meets your requirements. Next, choose a model that gets good mileage for its class. If you really need a roomy three-row SUV, for example, you could save an estimated $800 a year by choosing a 17-mpg Honda Pilot over a 12-mpg V8 Dodge Durango.

But here is a potential difference: While drivers of gas-powered cars may be able to save money by having an independent repair shop do the work, hybrid owners are more likely to rely on specially trained mechanics at the dealer.

Hybrids of Tomorrow

In the quest for better mileage, automakers are introducing hybrids that couple an electric motor with a diesel engine. Typically, diesel vehicles run up to 20 to 30 percent more efficiently than those burning gasoline, and a diesel hybrid can offer a similar advantage. These cars aren't without their drawbacks, however. Even though it's more efficient, diesel doesn't burn as cleanly as gasoline, and the cost of diesel engines and their exhaust treatments are higher than conventional gas engines. And while gas hybrid cars cost an average of about $3,000 more than conventional gas cars, diesel power can add $1,600 more to that figure. "You've got two very expensive technologies there," says Kyle Johnson, a spokesman for General Motors. "Is it economically viable? If there is a cost breakthrough or if fuel prices go through the roof, there could be potential there."

Plug-in hybrids are another approach. These are plugged in when parked and can travel a considerable distance on electric power alone before relying on a gas or diesel engine. For many around-town trips and commuting to work, these vehicles would need considerably less gas or diesel fuel. However, the size of the hybrid battery would need to be at least doubled, and current nickel-metal hydride batteries don't last long when used as a plug-in hybrid would use them. Whether large numbers of drivers would want to trade the hassle of plugging in a car for extra fuel economy remains to be seen.

The Hybridization of Hollywood

Is Leo the sign of the times? Film star Leonardo DiCaprio used to drive a massive Lincoln Navigator, then went hybrid. "I own a Toyota Prius; it's a step in the right direction," he is quoted as saying. "It's a gasoline-electric midsized car that gets about 50 miles per gallon. We have the technology to make every car produced in America today just as clean, cheap, and efficient."

Hybrids on the Horizon

For a look at new hybrids scheduled to appear on the market, check out CR's forecast of what's to come, by going to *www.ConsumerReports.org/energy* and clicking on New Hybrids.

ConsumerReports·org/energy

But diesel engines are up to 30 percent more efficient than gasoline engines, and they now seem to be enjoying a comeback, thanks to technological improvements that make them quicker and quieter, with cleaner performance. Another factor is a

OTHER TECHNOLOGIES, OTHER FUELS

While hybrids get most of the attention, other technologies show promise. It remains to be seen just what will be humming under the hood a decade or so from now. Diesel engines are nothing new: They've been around nearly as long as gas-powered cars. Though very popular in Europe, they haven't taken hold in the U.S. because older models had poor performance and a reputation for being difficult to start in cold weather, and they put off clouds of oily-smelling smoke.

The Volkswagen Jetta TDI is part of the new generation of cleaner-burning diesel vehicles.

federally mandated switch to low-sulfur fuel, due in fall 2006, which could make it possible to lower the emissions of future diesels to the levels of gasoline engines.

Biodiesel

It may be hard to believe, but you can run a diesel vehicle on the oil from a restaurant's deep-fat fryer. So-called biodiesel oils are vegetable- or animal-based, biodegradable, and capable of burning more cleanly than conventional petroleum-based diesel fuel. They can be produced here in North America from farm crops and recycled cooking oil, lessening the need for oil imports.

A diesel engine can run on straight vegetable oil or waste vegetable oil, but it requires modifications. Commercially produced biodiesel, made from soy or rapeseed oil, also requires some modification; but most current diesels can run on B5, which is 5 percent biodiesel and 95 percent conventional diesel. CR used a $795 kit from Greasecar Vegetable Fuel Systems that included a tank for the oil, hoses and fittings to warm the oil, and an inline filter to remove contaminants. The fuel was leftover oil picked up free from a local diner—most restaurants are glad to get rid of it—and it was strained through a paper paint filter to remove large food particles.

Installation of the kit is best left to a mechanic, unless you are a very competent do-it-yourselfer. And operating the vehicle isn't simple. The engine has to start off on regular diesel in order to warm the cooking oil, and it later is switched back to diesel just before shutting down to flush cooking oil from the fuel system. CR's test car ran as well on cooking oil as on diesel, and it accelerated as quickly, but on the highway it got 42 mpg compared to 45 with diesel.

If the oil doesn't cost you anything, a kit might pay for itself in a couple of years. But procuring and processing cooking oil is a lot of extra work for many motorists. You might also fill up with commercially available B5 fuel, the 5 percent biodiesel blend. It will work in any diesel engine without modification, costs about the same as regular diesel, and offers a good balance of performance, emissions level, and fuel economy. For now, it's sold mainly in the Midwest.

As the price of gasoline and diesel climb, there is more and more demand for alternative fuels. This Philadelphia company is set up to recycle spent restaurant grease into a cleaner-burning biodiesel.

The All-Electric Car

The all-electric car seems like such a good idea. You just plug it into a socket at home, the way you would a rechargeable flashlight. Electric cars have few moving parts—no cylinders, radiator, belts, or exhaust systems. Electrical systems are virtually nonpolluting (but only if you overlook the energy source that was used by the utility to generate the power). They are much more efficient than gas engines, making use of at least 75 percent of the energy they consume (but again, only if you overlook the inefficiencies of producing and transmitting electricity).

There are many limitations that have kept electrics from becoming commonplace. Recharging takes many hours, which is a considerable inconvenience. The batteries are heavy and expensive, with a range currently limited to between 40 and 120 miles on a charge. And if your battery runs low while you're out on the road, you would be stopped for hours at the next charging station, assuming a station was available. (That may be changing, however; California and Arizona now have some shopping malls, stores, and hotels that are equipped with chargers for their customers.) Finally, batteries have a limited life, and the EPA estimates the replacement cost at a hefty $8,000. With the advent of hybrids, major automakers have discontinued the production of electric cars.

Hydrogen Fuel Cells: Clean but Costly

The hydrogen-powered fuel cell has been one of those panaceas of automotive power for some time—but only in the lab until recently. Now a few car manufacturers have fleets of hydrogen-fuel-cell vehicles running around the world. A fuel cell generates electrical power somewhat like a battery. In a chemical reaction, stored hydrogen interacts with oxygen taken from the air to produce electricity for the vehicle's motor. Fuel cells operate at an efficiency of 40 to 70 percent, and the waste products are remarkably pure: water and heat.

Automakers are trying to harness the technology in a practical form, but cars running on fuel cells aren't likely to be widely available to consumers for many years to come. Hydrogen fuel is difficult to produce and to transport. The most efficient

> *Automakers are trying to harness the technology in a practical form, but cars running on fuel cells aren't likely to be widely available to consumers for decades.*

way of distributing it is as a highly compressed liquid, but liquefying hydrogen adds greatly to the cost of the fuel. And while hydrogen can be carried as a highly pressurized gas, the transportation costs are higher, too. Then there's the matter of the source for hydrogen: Although this element is found commonly in nature, the most cost-effective way to produce it happens to be from natural gas, and tapping this source wouldn't ease our reliance on fossil fuels. Also, there will have to be some way of making hydrogen available to motorists across the country. California plans to take the lead with its Hydrogen Highway Network initiative, which would set up hydrogen filling stations along many of the state's highways by 2010. Similar programs have been proposed for regions of Canada.

The Honda FCX is the world's first production fuel-cell vehicle. Like other fuel-cell prototypes, the Honda FCX is a zero-emissions car, producing only

The Honda FCX is a pioneering attempt to come up with a practical fuel-cell vehicle.

water as exhaust. As of this writing, the FCX was being leased only for fleet use by select utilities and municipalities and one California family for evaluation purposes.

TECHNOLOGY: TEACHING THE GAS ENGINE NEW TRICKS

The venerable gasoline-fueled internal-combustion engine isn't dead yet. A number of new adaptations may extend the life of this tried-and-true motor.

With variable valve timing, a sensor detects the engine's speed so that valves open and close in a way that maximizes torque and power at all speeds and in various driving conditions. Compared with a typical engine with fixed timing, a vehicle with variable valve timing might be 5 percent more efficient. Direct fuel injection of gasoline will improve performance and fuel economy by adjusting the air-and-fuel mixture based on the engine's demand, potentially increasing efficiency by 12 percent. Over the lifetime of the vehicle, that might add up to a total savings of $3,200. And there will be further development of the variable displacement engine, which does the neat trick of deactivating cylinders when less power is needed. In effect, an eight-cylinder engine could temporarily operate on just four. By running on fewer cylinders, a vehicle can potentially cut its energy needs by 7 percent or more.

Renewable Fuels

A potentially promising way to ease our dependence on drilling for oil is to grow our own fuel

■ Save with Off-Brand Gas

Don't get hung up on buying only nationally known brands of gas. Low-priced brands usually are identical to the gas sold at franchised gas stations.

Station Locations

A challenge in driving an alternative-fuel vehicle is finding a place to fill 'er up. For help in finding alternative fuels, go to *www.Consumer Reports.org/energy* and click on Where to Get Alternative Fuels. No matter what you need—electric, natural gas, propane, biodiesel, ethanol, hydrogen—this Web site shows where to go. That's assuming that a source exists in your area, of course. As of this writing, for example, a search for hydrogen within 25 miles of Philadelphia came up empty.

ConsumerReports.org/energy

domestically. Certain agricultural crops and other biomass, like switchgrass, cornstalks, and wood pulp, can be converted into ethanol (ethyl alcohol), which already is often added to gasoline for cleaner burning. Most ethanol fuel in the U.S. is made from corn and is sold in the Midwest. The standard blend is E85, consisting of 85 percent ethanol and 15 percent gasoline. E85 requires specially manufactured engines, and it delivers about 30 percent fewer miles per gallon than gasoline. Ethanol's lower fuel economy also results in more CO_2 emissions than a similar gasoline vehicle, although ethanol advocates say that there is no net increase because the plants used to grow crops for the fuel absorb as much CO_2 as the cars burning it emit. E10, which is commonly available, contains just 10 percent ethanol and is used to lower emissions where air pollution is a particular concern. Vehicles can burn it without special modification.

DaimlerChrysler, Ford, and GM offer a number of "flexible-fuel" cars and trucks that can run on E85 and gasoline in any combination. The engines and fuel systems have to be altered to compensate for alcohol's corrosive effect, and a sensor adjusts the fuel injection and timing by detecting the percentages of the fuel mixture.

INDEX